Peaceful Mind

by John Burke

Masters Series
Guide to Kata & Bunkai

Karate Academy
- 2005 -

© John Burke 2005

First published in Great Britain in 2005 by
Martial Arts World Ltd,
Newton Abbot, Devon, TQ12 2RX

Peaceful Mind
By John Burke

Published by
Karate Academy Ltd
8 Signal Buildings, Brunel Road, Newton Abbot, Devon, TQ12 4PB, England

Printed and Bound in Great Britain.

British Library Cataloguing in Publication
Data available

ISBN 0955034035

Warning:
Martial Arts can be dangerous. Practice should not be undertaken without first consulting your physician. Training should take place under the supervision of a qualified instructor. The contents of this book are for educational use and in no way do we endorse the use of the techniques herein. Practitioners need to be aware of the Law and how it pertains to "Use of Reasonable Force" in cases of self-defence. Remember, ignorance does not equate with innocence.

PEACEFUL MIND

Acknowledgements:
Everyone we meet adds to our perception of the world around us;
everyone we meet adds to our understanding of the Martial Arts.
Special thanks must go to our Instructors over the years,
including (in chronological order)
our parents,
Peter Maduro, Jim Harvey, Yoshinobu Ohta, Keinosuke Enoeda,
Phil Trebilcock, George Dillman, Leon Jay,
Patrick McCarthy, Russell Stutely, Rick Moneymaker, Anthony Blades,
Peter Holmes, Eddie Stokes, Tom Muncy, Ron Van Browning,
Martyn Harris, Neil Ellison & Stuart Howe.

Photographs by
Clare Potter

Special Thanks: The martial artists who appear in this guide are students and helpers at Eikoku Karate-do Kei-kokai. They did not ask to appear in here, but were prepared to pose at great risk to their self-esteem. *Mike Daniels, Paul Wilson, Thank You.*

Also available:

A Karate Primer

Eikoku Karate-do Keikokai Grading
Syllabus

Fortress Storming—the masters series
guide to Bassai Dai kata & bunkai

...and the dvd series which accompa-
nies both the grading syllabus and the
Kata & Application volumes

Please see
www.johnburke.info
For details.

Contents

Please note:
The following forewords are presented in order
of the Dan grade of the authors.
I have huge respect for each of these people, and
so placing them in any other order would have
been to ascribe an importance that might have
misrepresented what they have individually done
for me.
We can argue about what a grade means over a
drink, but I can't place any of these people *first*
in terms other than the way they are recognised
by their Dan.

This author thoroughly recommends training
with any and all of the foreword writers.

Foreword

Once a closely guarded secret practice, *kata* is the reason karate, as an art, has been preserved and passed down to this day.
Its heritage can be traced back to the Chinese progenitors of
quanfa. Sadly, however, the unique formula once used to help
deliver the contextual intentions culminated in kata was lost in
the wake of the modernization of the original art. It can be ar-
gued that the North Asian, Confucian-based pedagogy is partially responsible for the widespread confusion in relation to kata.
Specifically, a culture of learning and replicating "the classics",
rather than understanding them results in a gradual degradation
of meaning. The result, when coupled with the cultural mystique
surrounding the martial arts, has been a lack of recognition con-
cerning the most logical scenarios addressed by kata.

In 1985, after nearly twenty years of study, I became discour-
aged by the modern interpretation of kata and its incongruous
kata practices. A pivotal point in my training I journeyed to Japan in search of a teacher, a style, or even an organization
which could mentor me in a more rational, coherent and systematized manner. Specifically, I was looking for someone who
could; #1.Use realistic acts of physical violence as a contextual
premise from which to learn [rather than the 3K rule-bound reverse punch scenarios], #2. Employ practical two-person drills
to recreate those realistic acts of physical violence found in today's society and provide prescribed defensive templates ultimately leading to functional proficiency, #3. Show how the prescribed templates [i.e. the composites which make up kata] not
only culminated the lessons already imparted but, when linked
together, clearly offered something greater than the sum total of
their individual parts [i.e. kata], and finally, #4. To possess the
ability to clearly demonstrate where these prescribed templates

[mnemonic mechanisms] existed in the classical/ancestral-based kata and how they were linked back to both generic and specific acts of physical violence. While there was certainly no shortage of excellent yudansha everywhere I looked during my decade in Japan, I found no trace of such teachings anywhere there, Okinawa or beyond!

Traveling to Okinawa, Fuzhou, the Shaolin Temple and other sources of origin, my meeting and cross-training with many of the most senior authorities of karate and quanfa had unequivocally disclosed not only just how nebulous the art was but also how incongruous its application practices had become. Perhaps in theory this may functioned well, especially against passive resistance within the protected environment of one's dojo, but, against the active resistance of unmitigated physical violence, such practices, as far as I am concerned, were naive. Trying to make sense of out that experience I was compelled to make my own deductions which ultimately resulted in the establishment of the HAPV-theory [Habitual Acts of Physical Violence] and two-person drill concepts.

In the years which followed I took the lead in promoting functional kata application practices when I established a study group [the International Ryukyu Karate-jutsu Research Society] and began to build small bridges by uniting other like-minded learners all over the world. To help greet the disdain that my *"different"* interpretations would most certainly meet I not only reminded seniors of Dr. John Ray's advice [that *"Contempt prior to full investigation enslaves a person to ignorance"*] but also quoted Albert Einstein [*"We cannot solve our problems with the same level of thinking that created them"*]. I knew that thinking-outside-the-box was not only necessary it was the only acceptable way seniors could break free from the of narrow-mindset which prevails in our tradition. To help deliver the functionally effective application practices I was presenting, I offered morsels of historical testimony wrapped in applied science [common mechanics] supported by immutable principles. Moreover, to help resolve any moral and or conceptual misunderstandings I leaned heavily upon the venerable wisdom of Zen prelate, Matsuo Basho [*"Choosing not to follow in the footsteps of the old masters but rather to seek what they sought,"*] and the insights of Marcel Proust [*"The real voyage of discovery consists not in seeking new lands, but in seeing with* new eyes"]. In the years which have since past not only has the HAPV-theory and concept of two-person drills been widely accepted, the issue that styles can be best explained through understanding this phenomena has also given rise to a new movement from which many new researchers have come.

One such researcher to surface at the forefront of this movement is John Burke of the United Kingdom. A fine example of eclecticism John has studied the work of today's leading experts and gone on to present his own findings. I have enjoyed many opportunities of working with this young sensei in the more than 5 years that he's been a member of our group. Not only am I impressed with his unfaltering passion for the history of the art but equally impressive is his physical skill and penchant for organizing a systematized method of learning Shotokan kata application practices, as exampled in this publication. If you were impressed with the format of his first book, "*Fortress Storming*," then I am certain that you'll find this complimentary text, "*Peaceful Mind*," a welcome addition to that information.

I'd like to congratulate John on the publication of this wonderful work and thank him for another important contribution to our tradition. Such a contribution, not just to Shotokan, but to the entire karate community in the UK and beyond, is the benchmark that sets him apart from others. John Burke is a credit to our industry and I am proud to be associated with people like him and I hope you'll enjoy this book as much as I have.

Kind regards

_____

Patrick McCarthy
Hanshi 8th Dan
International Ryukyu Karate-jutsu Research Society
http://www.koryu-uchinadi.com

Foreword

I can sum up the latest work from John Burke quite simply; peaceful mind from a brilliant mind...

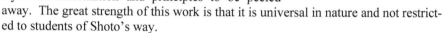

The Heian kata are quite often overlooked – something that the student will trawl through very early on in their journey. This work serves to refocus the importance of their study, not just for junior grades, but also for experienced black belts.

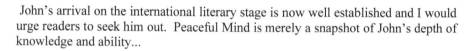

Peaceful Mind equips the reader with a thorough technical and historical grounding as well as many layers of information and principles to be peeled away. The great strength of this work is that it is universal in nature and not restricted to students of Shoto's way.

John's arrival on the international literary stage is now well established and I would urge readers to seek him out. Peaceful Mind is merely a snapshot of John's depth of knowledge and ability...

If you think you "know" the Heian kata, think again.

Anthony Blades
6th dan
27th August 2006

Foreword

I have known John Burke for about 12 years now and have seen him grow in stature at an amazing rate throughout the Martial Arts Community.

His extensive research into the true meaning of Kata Bunkai is at the forefront of today's knowledge base. Following on from his previous work "Fortress Storming" his new book, "Peaceful Mind" is a superb account of how the Heians / Pinans should be utilised within your own Martial Arts training.

This book has everything that the Karate-ka requires to truly begin to understand how and why Kata should work.

Explained in easy to understand terms this book is ideal for both Student and Instructor alike.

On my first reading of the first few chapters of this book I was compelled to call John and let him know just how superb his new book really is. I am sent various works both on tape and in book format by many Martial Artists all over the world for my opinions. Rarely do I ever write a foreword and even more rare is it that I am excited about the work I see or read. In the case of John's new book I was both excited and offered to write a foreword.

I can pay this book no higher compliment than to order a copy myself and to make it available on my website.

Well done again, John. Another superb addition to your ever expanding range.

Russell Stutely
6th Dan Karate
Co-founder Open Circle Fighting Method
OCFM International Coach
6th Dan OCFM
BCA Senior Coach
4th Dan Kickboxing
3rd Dan Torite Jutsu
Boxing Coach
Combat Hall of Fame
Columnist for the UK's leading Martial Arts Magazines
Fighters Trainer
Europe's leading authority on the use of Pressure Points in the Martial Arts

July 2006

Foreword

John Burke and I have much in common in our approach to karate training. It is therefore a pleasure and an honour to write this foreword for John's exploration of the Heian (Pinan) kata series, "Peaceful Mind".

I first met John Burke sensei several years ago at his Paignton Dojo, since then we have become firm friends and I have had the pleasure of training and teaching alongside him many times. Burke sensei is an excellent martial artist who has a genuine love for and interest in his art. His teachings maintain the traditions of Shotokan Karate with an emphasis on effective application of the principles and techniques inherent in kata as workable self defence.

I am sure that this work will open doors for both beginners and experienced martial artists alike, irrespective of style, and I know that "Peaceful Mind" will reflect favourably on John Burke, his students and his instructors.

Martyn Harris,
4th Dan Ryukyu Kempo,
Founder Red Dragon Karate Institute
July 2006

Introduction

This book is about the heart of Karate training—kata!
Kata remain one of the most misunderstood facets of the martial arts. Seen by many as being without use, sweeping statements are often made by accomplished martial artists:
"Learning kata just teaches you how to do kata."
"Kata doesn't teach you anything about combat."
Some *realists* have even gone so far as to stop teaching kata, or have made up their own "fighting kata" to more accurately resemble combative situations as they perceive them.

In order to honestly teach a kata, one must have an understanding of where the kata comes from and it's reason for being. Patrick McCarthy Hanshi often likens this to trying to learn a song in a foreign language. It may sound pretty but without it's context, translation, and understanding, it is ultimately meaningless.

I have made it my life's study to investigate kata—the principles and qualities which unite *all* kata - you see, in understanding the principles at the heart of Karate we can come to understand the whole of martial arts practice. There is a world of difference between understanding kata and making kata look nice.

There is nothing wrong with learning a kata for competition and making it as pretty as you can, but to then go on and teach that method as the "right" way to perform it is, in my opinion incorrect.

Each Kata shows us the creator's view of what self defence looks like. In this case we are looking at the five kata that make up the Heian family of kata; and we are analysing what the group of kata have to teach us.

If you have any realisations or any questions, honest students are always welcome at my dojo or at the seminars that I teach. There is nothing to be lost from asking the questions in person.

Come and train.

John Burke
Devon, UK, 2006

The Meaning of Karate

Karate as a martial art is seen in many forms. There are sports practitioners who use their art to better themselves physically and to drive them on towards competitive aspirations. There are those who see Karate only as a tool for defining their character —"Forging the Sword". Some Karate-ka (practitioners) will only have the art as a method of getting fit, and some will see it only as an interesting hobby; perhaps an alternative to the modern cluttered, western lifestyle. It may even be seen as a business by those teaching classes, seminars, and making dvds and books.

Karate may be many things, but at it's heart; at it's origin; it existed to protect people from those who would do them harm.

The practice of Karate is usually divided into 3 sections; Kihon: the practice of basic techniques and combinations; Kata: the practice of set patterns or forms of formal exercise; and Kumite; matching hands—a way of sparring.

The kata movements are often taught as something that one has to learn to obtain their next grade, and sometimes there are no meanings taught for these movements.

In this book, I will show applications to the movements beyond the simple versions shown in many classes that revolve around kumite style movements. That type of *bunkai* (analysis) serves to drive the practitioner into a performance that requires dynamism and clear reaction times. The type of bunkai that relies upon Karate-style attacks does a good job of preparing a practitioner for performance, but does not prepare us for self-defence situations.

The applications shown here share some common themes—the primary one being "You cannot practice this movement with full speed and power on a training partner or you will injure them." This is proof of the necessity of kata.

These are not necessarily the most sophisticated bunkai, but they are techniques which will introduce the reader to the principles which govern all kata movements and their *oyo jutsu* (application skills).

Once you have applications, you can practice kata with speed and power—making sure that you visualise the effects and events precisely in order to condition your mind *and* body.

The Meaning of Kata

The term "*kata*" is usually translated as "*form*", or "*pattern*". In Japan there are many things that have kata. Not just martial arts, but in every day life. You might think of it like having good manners; there is a right and a wrong way of doing things. People practice doing things "the right way", and this is practicing a kata—having good form.

There is a right way to hand over a business card to someone you respect, and there is a right way to receive it. This is a kata. Another way of putting it would be "ritual", and in the same way that a ritual can become devoid of meaning, so too can kata if they are not upheld as a full tradition. When parts of the ritual are not understood, the whole ritual loses its potency.

Kata itself can be written in a couple of different ways. The first way is the usual way, and it indicates, in the way that only a pictogram can, that something has been engraved in the ground. It shows that there is furrow and this is something that must be fitted into, not something that you make fit you.

Kata = style

The second way of writing kata indicates a shape that is a basis. A form that is an initial idea. If you write your kata this way then there is always room for individual interpretation.

Either way, kata act as a database of techniques. They are the storehouse of knowledge, like a computer programme. However, if you stare blankly at computer data like I do then it doesn't mean anything to you. You must understand the context that it was written in and what the intention of the writer was before it can make sense. You must understand how to take it apart again (*bunkai*).

Kata = form

Kata act as a memory aid. A physical book to promote muscle-memory rather than just a written book that might help you learn visually but does nothing for the kinaesthetic learner.

Karate kata hold the vital responses to unwarranted acts of aggression. They do not feature the verbal pre-amble or distraction techniques nor the study of one's surroundings that are necessary to remain safe, just the responses once a confrontation has begun to get physical.

This study guide is to remind practitioners of the Heian kata, how they look, and how to get the best out of them. No book can take the place of training with a qualified instructor. Your instructor is there to guide you in not only how the kata looks but in how you should feel when you perform it, and even what thoughts should be in your head. A book can tell you these things, but cannot check that it is being carried out correctly.

At the same time, no instructor can be with you *all* the time, so books and videos serve a useful purpose. There is also something to be said for discovering information for one's self. Information earned by searching for it is usually more highly prized than information given.

The Heian kata are generally taught to kyu grade students to pass from one coloured belt to another. In successful Dan (black belt) grading examinations they will usually also be called upon to cement a positive decision.

The version shown within heralds from *Shotokan*, nominally the style of **Funakoshi Gichin**, credited by many as the father of modern karate-do. Modern Karate-do, it is often said, differs from it's earlier ancestors in that movements have been lost or hidden. Certainly, many movements within Shotokan kata have become homogenised and made safe for practice by school children. This does not mean that the old, dangerous techniques are removed; just that the dangerous answers have been overlooked in favour of simplistic explainations favouring the aesthetic required for competition. Anyone who has seen (or been in) a real confrontation will attest that it is far from pretty, yet modern kata competition requires a beauty in motion akin to Olympic gymnastics to score winning points.

The Heian kata (plural pronunciation of words is the same as singular in Japanese) are performed in different ways by different associations. In essence though, the moves are the same. The differences will usually be about an exact position of a hand or foot, or a slight change in timing of performance.

More important than which version is shown here are the priciples espoused, which are universal. They apply to all kata and all martial arts.

Principles can be broken down into what is useful for performance (*embu*), what is important for health and exercise, and what is important for combat. These things are not always the same. **Itosu Ankoh** listed in his "10 Articles" to the government interested in introducing Karate into the Okinawan School system

"7. In karate training one must determine whether the specific application is suitable for defence or for cultivating the body."

(as translated by Hanshi Patrick McCarthy).

Performance Principles:

Below are listed the published thoughts of some of Karate's great masters. First is **Master Funakoshi**, from whom we trace all Shotokan Karate:

Three Cardinal Points:
i)   Light and Heavy application of Strength.
ii)   Expansion and Contraction of the body.
iii)   Fast and Slow movements of the body.

The elements that must be considered during kata practice are

1.   **Ikita Kata.** Feeling and purpose. Alive.

2.   **Inen.** Spirit.

3.   **Chikara no Kyojaku.** Proper application of power. Technique can be strong or yielding, hard then soft.

4.   **Waza no Kankyu.** Variations in the timing of movement, sometimes fast, sometimes slow.

5.   **Kisoku no Donto.** Rhythm of breathing, when to inhale and exhale.

6.   **Balance.** Proper balance must be maintained in the performance of Kata.

Than we come to Master Kanazawa. Kanazawa is one of the great instructors who were given the chance to spread shotokan throughout the world. He is re-nown for his flexibility and his breaking displays in the 1960s. Master Kanazawa is the head of one of the largest Shotokan groups around.

Kanazawa's 10 rules:

Yoi no kisin	The spirit of being ready.
Inyo	The contrast and transition of active and passive
Chikara no kyojaku	The degree of Power. Where you put your strength.
Waza no kankyu	The speed of the technique
Tai no shinshuku	The degree of expansion and contraction.
Kokyu	Breathing.
Tyakugan	The points to aim for.

Kiai	Spirit Shout. Everything together.
Keitai no hoji	The correct positioning.
Zanshin	Remaining awareness.

Practitioners will note that these masters are concerned with not only how a kata *looks*, but also how important it is to understand what the moves are *for!*

The famous Karate master **Oyama Masutatsu**, whose school was known for it's fierce fighting, was known to have said "Kata is the soul of Karate".

BACKGROUND

The Heian family of 5 kata are predominant in the **Shotokan** style of Karate-do. This is nominally the style of **Funakoshi Gichin**, and it was he who is formally credited with introducing Karate to Japan in the 1920s.

Funakoshi did not believe that Karate should have "styles". There was only Karate, not my karate or your karate, just karate. It was not Funakoshi who named Shotokan. The name comes from the building that was built for Funakoshi to teach from which was destroyed during World War II. Funakoshi's students named the hall, and they began to refer to what they were doing, colloquially, by the same name. Once the master had died it was the biggest organisation that made the name popular. It has stuck, despite the fact that we practice differently from the type of practice that actually took place at "the Shotokan".

> "Shoto" was Master Funakoshi's pen-name for his poetry writing. It means "waving pines". "Kan" means "hall". The shotokan was the hall of waving pines.

Funakoshi's teacher was **Itosu Ankho**, and it was he who formulated the Heian kata. The kata are commonly known as Heian Shodan, Heian Nidan, Heian Sandan, Heian yondan and Heian Godan.

Heiwa

Antei

Heian is the contraction of the term for the reading of the characters **Heiwa** and **Antei**.

Heiwa means *peace* and *harmony*. Antei means *stability* and *composure*.

Heian is commonly translated as "*Peaceful Mind*". None of the characters that make up the term have the symbol for "Mind" in them, so a more correct translation might be "*Tranquillity* Level One" for Heian Shodan etc. Heian/pinan can be taken to mean *Peace,* Tranquility, *Normal*...

Shodan might be taken to mean First Level or First Degree, and the numbers continue **Nidan**, **Sandan**, **Yondan** and **Godan**.

The Okinawan reading of the character "Hei" is pronounced "Pin", so some schools label the kata series as **Pinan** Shodan -Godan.

The Heian kata would appear to have originated at the turn of the 1800s into 1900s. It was at this time that Itosu sensei lobbied the government to have

Heian

Karate adopted as formal exercise classes in schools. In a letter dated 1908 Itosu sensei asked the government to consider the benefits of Karate training to include the increase in determination, physical fitness, and the development of good citizens. He postulated that these citizens would be extremely useful to the Japanese drive towards a strong army.

The series of kata, numbering five in total, were due to be taught in the Okinawan secondary schools. The original sequence began with what Shotokan practitioners refer to as Heian Nidan. This kata used to be called Pinan Shodan.

Shodan	初段
Nidan	二段
Sandan	三段
Yondan	四段
Godan	五段

In many places Pinan Shodan is taught after Pinan Nidan (the Shotokan Heian Shodan) due to the complexity of the "first" kata. This means that they teach Pinan Nidan (Heian Shodan), then Pinan Shodan (Heian Nidan), before proceeding with the rest in order. This is the same order we teach them in, but in their numbering system they are learning Level 2, then Level 1!

Funakoshi is known to have changed the sequence in order to make it easier to learn for students.

The family of kata are usually said to be from **Shuri-te** lineage, meaning that they originated in or around the town of Shuri—once the capital of Okinawa. They are also said to be "*Shorin*" in their performance; meaning that they are full of light, fast movements, rather than those that rely on body-weight and strength.

Common knowledge has it that the Heian/

The number **five** has a significance to oriental people as a fortunate number. Observe the number as part of the medicinal Five Elements and in **Musashi**'s Book of Five Realms. It is considered a lucky number in Japan, but also one that is common in nature. One only has to observe the usual five fingers and toes on each limb. Indeed, if one observes the head to be similar to a limb, then there are 5 extremities to the body.

Pinan kata come from Itosu, but there was some controversy over who taught them to Funakoshi. When Funakoshi was learning, common knowledge has it that he began with the **Tekki** kata, and later learned **Bassai** and **Kanku** in their older forms (Passai and Kusanku).

One account has it that Master Funakoshi picked up the Heian kata from **Mabuni Kenwa** sensei on a visit to Osaka sometime in the 1920s. Funakoshi was known to have made several visits to Mabuni and other teachers in order to learn additional facets of the art. During these visits he took with him his son, Yoshitaka, and Nakayama Masotoshi to learn other kata which were not originally considered to be part of the Shotokan canon. Mabuni is known as the founder of **Shito-ryu**; and Funakoshi's humility in learning from a fellow student (his junior) is noteworthy.

It is by no means certain that Funakoshi received the Heian kata this way, however, as other recollections have Funakoshi known as *"the Pinan sensei"* as it was "all he ever taught" in the early days. Even though Funakoshi might not have formally been one of Itosu's students in his teaching days on Okinawa, it's not too far fetched to believe that he might have picked up these important "new" kata from his teacher when it became known that they would be introduced into schools. Most commonly, it is said that Funakoshi learned the Pinan kata from Itosu.

A certain era of Japanese history was known as the "Heian Period". This time extended from **794 – 1185AD.** It was a noteworthy period of history in that, in Japan, many of the advances in politics, art, and industry are considered to have their roots in this time. It is the time just before the feudal period which made Japan a nation at civil war for so long.

Some historians have investigated the theory that Itosu did not create the Heian series from scratch, but instead modified existing kata. Most people agree that they can see **Jion** and **Kanku Dai** amid the movements in the Heian kata, but some believe that there was another pair of forms which might have served as a basis.

The Channan Hypothesis:

There is much confusion and speculation over the idea that the 5 kata might find their origins in earlier kata known as "Channan". The greatest difficulty with this is that no-one really practices the Channan kata of that time. Various experts have concocted theories about what the Channan kata *might* have looked like, but no-one knows for sure.

One story goes: the village of **Channan** is rumoured to have originated a "village art" which was encoded as forms Channan Dai and Channan Sho. This theme recurs in the roots of Karate, and the traditional Okinawan village dances tend to look very much like movements from Kata. Village dances were not just something for women, but a noble art-form in themselves; often practised by the *Shizoku* class (similar to the Samurai of Japan).

However, there is also the possibility that the (in)famous "shipwrecked sailor" theory might have a part to play. Most people have hear the story that a Chinese sailor became shipwrecked on Okinawa and as thanks for being spared/saved/cared for taught obscure Chinese kata (*hsing*) to various Okinawan martial artists. This story has problems in that the martial artists in question worked, mostly, for the royal court and it would have been easy for them to hand over a poor soul in trouble to Chinese authorities on the island who could have gotten him home safely. Anyway, this sailor was said to have come from Nan'an, and it is highly likely that the Chinese name became Annan and maybe even Channan in the Okinawan tongue. There is another kata known as Annan.

When one studies the "higher kata" they are often found in pairs. These are often termed "*Dai*" (or major version), and "*Sho*" (or minor version). Often these kata contain similar movements, but are divided due to the respective finesse or "size" of the movements, or some other factor that makes one of them "major" and the other "minor".

Just for a moment it might be fun to play with performing Heian Nidan and Heian Shodan as one kata and then comparing the result with performing Heian Yondan and Heian Sandan as a second kata. Could the result be something like Channan Dai and Channan Sho? It would certainly seem to fit with the *Large Movement Dai kata, Small Movement Sho kata* way of thinking!

This would leave Heian Godan as a totally Itosu creation, demonstrating why it looks nothing like the others!

Yet another tale tells of Itosu being taught a kata by **Chaing Nan**, a Chinese martial artist from Tomari. It must be remembered that a significant proportion of Okinawans were, in fact, Chinese. The islands collectively known as "The Ryukyu Chain" (of which Okinawa is the largest) lie between the southern tip of Japanese Kyushu island and China. As such, they were a great "melting pot" for all the local cultures. Many times in their history, the Ryukyus were "officially" conquered by the Japanese, then the Chinese, and back again. These "wins" were usually political, and involved the paying of tribute to the "conquering" government. Okinawa, being only some 40 miles square, is far too small to raise an army to fend off a whole nation, but they paid tribute and taxes to the *nation-du-jour*.

Due to the secretive nature of the early Karate-ka and the bombing of Okinawa during World War 2, there really are no proper records of the kata, their names, and their origins. No-one really knows the truth, and as such all we have are opinions and educated guesses.

Using the "Ockham's Razor" way of thinking, we are taught to take the simplest route to our conclusions.

In **794AD**, in order to insulate it against the growing influence of Buddhist clergy at Nara, **Emperor Kammu** chose to relocate the Japanese capital city to **Heian-kyo**. This is the site of modern day Kyoto. The old city, like much of Japanese heritage, was modelled on Chinese influences. These included **Chang'an**, the capital city of the **Tang Dynasty**, in China. Chang'an is the modern day Xi'an. Heian-kyo was the capital of Japan until the Meiji Restoration caused the relocation in 1868 to Edo (modern Tokyo). 1868 is also the year that master Funakoshi was born.

Isn't Channan the same as Chang'an? We're aware of the Heian period of history and now it seems that the period had a city that shared it's name. That city was based on another city: Chang'an! It seems logical, then, to say that Heian kata were based on techniques that came out of Chang'an in China. It is no secret that the old name for *The Way of the Empty Hand* was **Tang Hand**. The Tang capital was copied by the Japanese and the Tang techniques were renamed suitably for the historical reflection.

Sakagami Ryusho (1915-1993) considered himself to be the 3rd generation inheritor of Itosu's karate. He posited that the origins of the Channan kata can be found in **General Ch'i Chi-kuang**'s book **Chi-hsiao Hsin-shu**. This heralds from Ming dynasty China (after the Heian period).

Ch'i Chi-kuang was born Lu-chiao in Shantung province on 10th January 1528 (he died 17th January 1588). The Japanese reading for his name is **Seki Keiko**. Chi-kuang's family had served the Ming dynasty for 6 generations. This meant that was automatically a General. Legend has it that he trained at the **Shaolin** temple and it's possible as he served all over China. His book translates as *The New Treatise on the Disciplined Service* and was published in 1562. In the main, this book is about military strategy and tactics. However, chapter 14 is about empty hand techniques. 32 positions are listed, including "Flag & Drum"; "The Winding Arm"; "Carrying A Cannon at the Head" and "Riding a Tiger". These postures look very similar to movements found in the Heian kata.

T'ai-tzu Ch'ang Chuan is the name of the fighting method of developed by **Emperor T'ai-tzu** (formerly general Chao K'uang-yin). He was the first emperor of the Sung dynasty (960-1279AD), and reigned 960-976, during the Heian period, but in China.
The Emperor's *Ch'ang Chuan* is "*long boxing*", and could be a compound of *CHi-kuANG*. So we have a method of long boxing (Shorin-ryu/Shurite/Shotokan is known for expansive movements). We have a noble link to China in the Heian period, and we have a reason for the name being

changed to reflect Japanese tastes but still reflecting the Chinese influence.

The names then, likely come not from any stranded sailors or village influences, but from the politics of Japan and the slightly sly word-play of Confucian-educated scholars like Funakoshi trying to surreptitiously maintain the links to Karate's Chinese origins.

Notable martial artists such as **Hohan Soken** only taught Pinan Nidan and Sho-dan, leading some to say that these were the "original" kata, yet others taught Pinan one-four as they "come from Matsumura", stating that Godan was "no good" as it was only made recently. This helps to sustain the idea that this kata was created by Itosu. It seems a little harsh to suggest that a kata created by Itosu might be "no good".

Some say that the Heian series of kata are "watered down karate". Derided by many as being "basic", we urge all practitioners to think as though they were Itosu, creating a series of kata for the express purpose of training the youth, forging strong spirits. Wouldn't you use your best moves? Wouldn't you create technically demanding, stamina building exercises? It is certainly worth thinking that though some moves may have had hands clenched into fists for the protec-tion of the youth training in the kata, the original, open handed movements are not gone, they are still there for all who care to see them.

The key is that you must have some knowledge of where your art comes from and how it has been handed down. Once you accept the idea that the move-ments are not designed to take on another trained fighter, but instead were for use against the common thugs and brigands of lonely Okinawan footpaths then suddenly the applications can be found.

This kata is a database of techniques, and the techniques, whether they are from Channan, from China, or made by Itosu can be used effectively by an "effectively-minded" person.

Our aim is to show that these "basic" kata can be beautiful, demanding, powerful training methods.

Commonly taught as introductory kata, the family has small variations in the way it is taught within Shotokan, WadoRyu, ShitoRyu, and as the Pin Yan Poomse in certain Taekwondo associations. As stated before, the principles are universal.

Heian Shodan

平
安
初
段

HEIAN SHODAN

Peaceful Mind Level One.

This used to be the second of the 5 heian kata until Master Funakoshi changed the order.

Most Shotokan practitioners will already know Kihon kata when learning Heian Shodan, and Kihon is featured elsewhere for reference. Every application to Kihon kata can also be found in Heian Shodan.

This kata is similar in shape/layout to Kihon Kata, with the addition of Tettsui uchi - hammer fist, age uke, and shuto uke performed both on-line and at 45° to the line.

The kata uses a front stance—zenkutsudachi—for all but the last four moves (which are in back stance—kokutsudachi).

Bring the feet together and bow from the hips in a polite manner. With the feet still together, announce the name of the kata in a firm manner. The way you name your kata sets the tone for the performance. Bring the feet apart and make the "ready" position:

Sink the weight by bending the knees and prepare the arms as one does in Kihon Kata, looking to the left at the same time.

Step out into zenkutsu dachi and make gedan barai as in Kihon. The hips are in the "half-facing" *hanmi* position.

One of the common errors in performing the first move is that students "fall" into technique instead of lowering the body and projecting the force forwards from the hips.

Step forward and make oi zuki chudan as in Kihon Kata. It is important to keep the hips at the same height throughout the step. Hips and shoulders are square to the direction of facing, *shomen*, in all punches in this kata.

Look behind.

Turn 180° clockwise on the left foot by moving the right foot, as in Kihon Kata.

Black Belt tip: during the turn begin the "contraction" of the body ready for the gedan barai. This keeps your centre-line covered the whole time.

Make gedan barai as in Kihon kata.
Ensuring the tension of the right knee muscles, the right hip is pulled back, as the right arm is drawn across the body and upwards.. Any foot movement is separate and secondary to the hip movement. This is not a "step". The arm pulls across the body and raises in a move similar to age uke before
...descending to make *tetsui uchi* (hammer fist) to the same height as the bridge of the nose. The arm remains bent and the bottom of the fist is parallel to the ground. The right hip is pushed back in to resume zenkutsudachi in hanmi.

Step forward into zenkutsudachi making oi zuki chudan.

Look to the left. Turn 90° anticlockwise to the left and prepare the arms as in Kihon.
Step onto the main line of the embusen and make gedan barai as in Kihon Kata.

Step forward and make age uke.
Step forward and make age uke.
Step forward and make age uke. **Kiai.**
Look to the right

Pull the left hip sharply around anticlockwise and prepare the arms
...to make gedan barai in zenkutsudachi to the right, just as in Kihon Kata.
Step forward and make oi zuki chudan, as in Kihon Kata. Look over the right shoulder.

Pivot 180° clockwise on the left foot, bringing the feet together and preparing the arms then step out and make gedan barai, as in Kihon Kata.
Step forward into zenkutsudachi and make oi-zuki chudan, as in Kihon Kata. Look to the left.

Pull the left hip sharply back and prepare the arms, as in Kihon kata.

Step into the main embusen with the left leg and make gedan barai, as in Kihon Kata.

Step forward and make oi zuki chudan, as in Kihon Kata.

Step forward and make oi zuki chudan, as in Kihon Kata.

Step forward and make oi zuki chudan, as in Kihon Kata. **Kiai.**

Look to the right

Pull the left hip sharply up and turn 90° anticlockwise to the right, stepping out into kokutsu dachi whilst making shuto uke. Then Look 45° to the right.

Black Belt Tip: to prevent overbalancing while turning, bring the feet together and step out rather than swinging the leg wildly around.

 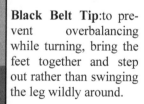

Step out at 45° to the previous line and make kokutsudachi and (right) shuto uke. Look to the right.

Pull the right hip back, pivot 135° clockwise on the left foot and step out into right leg kokutsu dachi and shuto uke.
Look 45° to the left. Step out at 45° to the previous line and make kokutsudachi and (left) shuto uke.
Yamae.
Naore.

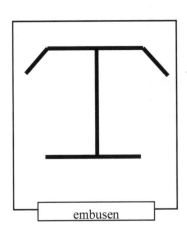

embusen

Applications

The movements of your kata each have meaning. They were originally put together to remind students of self-defence acts that they had practised before their teacher. There may be many applications for any one movement, and on our seminars we might teach slightly more advanced versions depending on which students are present.

For each movement to represent a self defence situation we will see that the types of situation reflect commonly occurring attacks.

Common themes in our applications include:

- Beginning at a range where there is a real danger of being struck by any of the attacker's weapons.
- Only using common methods of attack which an untrained attacker might reasonably be expected to use.
- Beginning at a casual guarded position rather than "in a stance".
- Making both hands work together—never leaving one hand "ready" or "pulling back to make the other hand more powerful".
- Making contact with the attacker half-way through the technique—not at the end.
- Penetration with each technique, not just surface contact.
- Leaving no gap between the attacker and our own body when seeking to control them.
- Co-ordination of Mind, Breath, and Body.

When analysing the pattern of attacks which occur "in the street" we see that there will usually be a pre-amble/"interview"/set-up/distraction which is verbal. The trained martial artist must recognise these factors and use it to raise his energy level from casual to "primed for action". This does not mean jump in to a full zenkutsudachi. Being ready is a state of mind—preparedness.

Common types of attack (which Patrick McCarthy Hanshi refers to as the **Habitual Acts of Physical Violence**) might include:

- Hook **punches**, straight punches, upper-cuts
- Single wrist **grab**, cross-body wrist grab, double wrist grab
- Grab at the forearm, elbow, or shoulder; either one-handed or two-handed
- **Pushing**, single-handed or two-handed from the front, side, or rear.
- Bear-hug grabs from the front, side, or rear; over the arms or under them.
- Strangulations/neck-grabs; one-handed, two-handed, from the front,

side, or rear
- Grabbing the groin.
- Head-**locks**; facing forwards or backwards
- Full-Nelson or half-Nelson locks from the rear, or Rugby tackle rushes from the front or side.
- Head-butt.
- Back-handed strikes, slaps
- Descending strikes or slaps
- **Kicks** to the shin or thigh
- Knee to the groin

The many variations on the above which may come from types of clothing or situation might also be investigated, but recognise the core principle: an assault is when one of the above methods enters within your personal space.

Recognise the attack's imminence and prepare to react to it. Know the effects of adrenaline and how they manifest. Have your plan ready and be prepared to see it through. As explained in the previous section; strikes from behind can only be deflected if you are psychic or there is some kind of warning (shadow/reflection/verbal abuse, etc.). If you manage to turn then it is no longer an attack from the rear.

The ground rules:

- **If you can avoid the confrontation, do.**

- **If you can talk your way out of it before it gets messy, do.**

- **If you can hit then escape, pre-emptively or otherwise, do.**

- **If you hit an attacker and it doesn't finish it then use the time you buy yourself to use your technique. An aggressor will be more compliant if you have already hit him.**

- **If one technique does not fulfill your requirements use another. Don't stop. Carry on until you are safe. Kata applications show a snap shot of action, not the whole fight.**

- **If you can, move to a position of relative safety/strength (off-line rather than directly in front of his "other" fist).**

- **Safety first. Practice the moves with speed, power, and visualisation only on a bag or thin air, not on a partner. This is what kata are for. When practicing on empty air don't lock out joints, use your muscles to stop the movement. When practising with a partner, start slowly and gently, and only increase the speed and intention with experience and to your partner's comfort threshold.**

The kata begins with a formal bow, and should be performed in the serious manner that this bow represents.

Sometimes, when students begin to look at applications, they imagine that there are applications to things like bowing. This is taking matters too far. With applications of Karate kata we must consider the social context that gave rise to the formation of the kata—these movements were not put together to deal with guns, and although the head-butt is one of a number of tools it was not common amongst Okinawan aristocracy as an initial greeting.

The bow is a sign of respect for the Japanese. It is not an indication of a secret "head-butt attack". The reason for the bow in a sword-wielding society was to expose the neck, thereby showing supreme trust in the person you bowed to. You literally gave them the possibility of taking your life. The English version of this would be to proffer your right hand, demonstrating that you are not about to draw your sword.

Let's take the view that the situation that the kata move responds to is unavoidable (if it could be avoided we would avoid it). Let's say that the start of the kata represents the early stages of a confrontation.

If we are to respond at all then we must have the capacity to do so. By this I mean that we must be programmed to "get over" the "flight or fight or freeze" syndrome that is natural and activate the mindset and techniques that we use in training.

This is why it is essential that realistic situations are re-enacted both with a partner (to identify targets and locations) and without a partner (kata practice) (to enable full power delivery of techniques).

Imagine the opponent is close. Talking hasn't worked and trying to walk away hasn't worked. For us to use the techniques we know we must believe that our life has been threatened. The level of response will be dictated by the level of threat.

The opponent reaches out and tries to grab our lapels. If we are fast enough to get them off then the following situation doesn't arise, but if they have shocked us with their language and attitude then they may well get to this event.

Gedan Barai

We: reach under their arms so that they cannot intercept our intention. If we reach across the top of the arms then the attacker will know that they are involved in "a fight" and will adjust their aggression and their response accordingly. Our aim is to see an end to the situation before " a fight" can materialise. Never confuse *a fight* with *protecting yourself*. They are contrary to each other.

Fearing a head-butt or knee strike, we need to disrupt their attention and their balance. We use our right hand to pull on their right elbow. Pulling sharply back towards our right hip causes the opponent to twist his body and momentarily look away, thus preventing a knee strike or a head-butt.

Principle
Distance. The attacker begins at a realistic distance to attack you, or they aren't actually attacking you.

Principle
Common Attacks. If the attack isn't the kind that people normally do then there is little reason to prepare for it. There are enough real types of attack for us to learn to deal with without creating fantasy ones.

Simultaneously we bring our left arm up across our body, above the attackers' arms. If the head-butt should slip through then he will "head" our arm. If our ascending fist happens to catch the attackers' jaw then we will count ourselves fortunate.

Our left arm then descends in a short arcing movement that goes across the throat of the attacker.

Where the severity of the attack is less, we can restrain ourselves to pushing down on the shoulder instead of striking the throat. Making a front stance prevents you from falling over when the opponent falls. It also makes use of the leg strength rather than relying on the strength of the arms.

Principle
Bodyweight. To use our bodyweight against someone is to add to our strength.
Thrusting bodyweight forwards is the use of a front stance.

Principle
Pre-emption. When you feel that there is no other alternative, then using what you know before the other person gets the chance to attack you might be all that you have.
It isn't necessarily a strike, though hitting pre-emptively might be sound advice.
The strike might be considered a stun, buying you time to do the technique that you favour; in which case we label it **BAR**—body alarm reaction.

Remember: an attacker may instinctively resist a push in a single direction, but a push in multiple directions on multiple planes is much harder to prevent.

Common errors in working this one with a partner include the "attacker" locking their arms straight. If they do this then they cannot attack you and as such you do not need to respond. If you did want to break the "straight arm" lock then a small distracting hit to the ribs or even up under the arms themselves would suffice.

The other major error is that the opponent doesn't get dropped to the floor. This is because the "defender" failed to give direction to the downward sweep of their arm, and so all it does is drag them around.

Principle
Multiple Angles. Taking a technique (any technique) through multiple angles and planes makes it more effective.

Principle
Both Hands Work. In every single technique, both hands have a function. No hand comes back to your body without something attached. If it's not *pulling*, leave it out in front.

Principle
Unite mind breath and body. Only with full intention, breathing and physical body will a technique come together to best effect.

Principle
Give a little to get a little. In order to pull someone who is very strong or resisting, it may be necessary to let them momentarily pull in their direction so that we can then pull in ours.

Oizuki Chudan.

By launching our body wholly forward we apply our body-weight to the punch. The strength of our legs is added to the strength of our arms.

By thrusting forward this way we launch onto the opponent. Our *hikite* pulls the opponent on to us so that *their* body-weight is also added to the punch.

We don't just magically attach to the opponent, but make our contact and stay in contact through the principles of *kake* and *muchimi*.

When these two factors work together, the strike will invariably bring the opponent down so that our chudan punch is located at their throat or face.

The version shown here takes a look at what happens if your gedan barai is only partially successful. Rather than struggle to finish the move, take advantage of the temporary and partial disruption to the attacker's balance by clearly ending the situation with a thrusting punch that also sends them away.

Principle
Adapt. Should one technique not succeed to the fullest extent then quickly move on to another. The idea of flow is paramount.

Principle
Redundancy. Even when the technique might not live up to your full expectations, it will serve a purpose.

Turning Gedan Barai.

When we analyse a kata, we may believe that turns are put there to create a nice geometric pattern for the sake of memorizing the set of moves.

It might be shocking, then, to see how the turn can be used as part of the technique.

With an attacker in front of you, you might well find yourself grabbed by the shoulders or arms.
Remember, the attacker has already gone through the psychological process of overcoming their fears to engage you; while you must still overcome yours. In order to even the odds, we like to put the attacker back in the same boat as us by giving them a shock.

Create BAR in the opponent with a reactive strike to buy compliance, then wrap your right arm around the back of their head, taking hold of shoulder or jaw.

There are solid reasons for using your right hand to do this. The first would be that it is usually a person's strong arm. The second would be that it is usually only opposed by an attacker's weak arm.

Going across the body (behind it) as we do, we will go a long way to preventing resistance as any subconscious anticipation will be favouring the left side of the attacker and we are going to affect them from their right!

Pulling with your arm is movement through one plane, so we give the technique angle and direction, enhancing it, by moving our body in a complete 180 degree turn, pivoting on our rearmost foot. With your left arm grabbing their right arm you create a base to turn them through.

Remember that the smaller the arc and the tighter the spiral, the more trouble the attacker will have with resisting your intention. Again we find that although someone can resist a push or pull on one plane, working through multiples disrupts any resistance.

Don't ignore the function of stance— the drive of bodyweight and effort in any given direction to maximise effect. It also really helps if the attacker's head hits your knee!

Once again, we must caution for care in practice. Turn sharply and this is a neckbreak. Turn gently and we have a throw over your hip.

You can see in the pictures that the defender has let go of the attacker's arm for their safety.

Principle
Balance. Everything you do must affect an attacker's balance while maintaining your own.
If the attacker is unbalanced they will not possess their full capability.

Tettsui Uchi

Grabbed by the right wrist, pull your hip away from the grabber. At the same time pull your hand across your body to free it.

It is important that the hip is pulled away from the attacker directly backwards. Any movement across the centre-line will reveal more targets on you than it hides, and will also put the attacker beyond the range of your weapons.

The wrist is freed by pulling through the opposable thumb of the attacker. Because you act fluidly and without tension they will be unable to stop you, no matter how strong they are. Small children can use this (once properly trained) to pull away from an adult!

As the fist rises, continue in a simple arc (that also keeps your centre-line covered) to descend onto the attacker's head.

Because the attacker has been pulled off balance by you removing their grip, you will usually find that your strike hits the "corner" of their head, where lots of delicate nerves lie.

If you fail to hit the corner because they haven't turned (sometimes, if their grip wasn't good or their arm was rigid with tension), then you will strike the forehead, the bridge of the nose, the jaw, the sternum, or perhaps even the shoulder.

As long as the strike is hard and "into" the body (not just striking the surface), then the exact target doesn't matter.

The hand that remains on the hip can remain there for a few reasons. Some of the applications that we practice have a static hand as an absolute necessity. In this situation we can see that as the attacker has grabbed us we could return the favour and grab them—keeping them stable at this point creates the base that we work around.

Principle
Soft & Hard, Targets & Weapons. Where the weapon you are using is bony, it should be used against soft targets. Where the weapon you are using is soft, it should be used against hard targets.
Placing hard weapons against hard targets usually leads to one of them getting broken—and it might be your weapon!
Soft weapons against soft targets leads to absorption of force in two directions, negating some of the effect.

Principle
Redundancy. Should your chosen technique only *half* succeed then you need to know that it will be *enough*. The best techniques are those that, should they miss their mark, still do what you intended.

Principle
Heavy Hand. All strike are designed to penetrate. Striking *through* a target is better than striking the surface.

Principle
Hand to your heart. Pulling your hand towards your heart is your strongest mechanical movement. Your whole body, every muscle, is made to *pull*. You don't have a pushing muscle. Pulling towards you has the added advantage of hyper-extending the grasp of anyone who has seized you.

Oi-zuki Chudan

The next punch can be taken to mean the same as previous punches.

Following on from the strike to the opponent's head, we can take hold.

Remember that even when you punch, as well as the bodyweight and legs being involved, you are using *two* hands.

The pulling *hikite* hand is used in this example to wrench the attacker's neck as you thrust the fist through their throat.

The *chudan* (middle) punch is once again shown to strike a *jodan* (top level) target; with the hikite being the reason for the height in the kata.

Turning Gedan Barai

Now, you could use the gedan barai in the same fashion as the previous times that it has been used.

The turn, in this case, is only 90 degrees to the left. Let's choose to give it a different reason.

Consider a cowardly attacker. They might choose to approach from your left because they suspect that, like most people, you are right handed. They also do not want to face your strong right hand. They might be wrong about your handedness, but it is a fair assumption.

The attack is initiated by the attacker placing their hand on your shoulder. Their intention is to pull you and turn you *into* their strike, thereby both multiplying the force of their strike and reducing your chances of coping by dizzying you. They would probably not use their right hand for anything other than this or to punch. We'll look at the left-hand variation further into this kata.

You cover your centre-line and drop your body-weight while at the same time making a BAR strike to the "corner" of the attacker's ribs, buying valuable time.

Covering the body this way also brings your arm out from under the attacker's direct control and into your "power-zone" - directly in front of your body.

As a fail-safe, if the attacker were to continue, our most vulnerable areas would be covered from "upper body" attacks.

This "covering up" is vital because it is a natural reaction. As such we should not wish it away, but rather channel it into becoming a useful part of every technique we know.

Too many martial artists train their "flinch reaction" away, when evolution has spent a long time training it into us!

Continue the movement by bringing your elbow and then your forearm down across the attacker's neck.

Don't overlook the downward nature of the elbow in making gedan barai. It begins the attacker's descent which you then accentuate with your forearm to drive them to the ground.

Age Uke

A repeated motif draws attention to the move, ensuring that we spend time learning it and practicing it. It can also indicate that there are multiple applications to the same technique, as well as allowing for a nice geometric configuration to help our learning of the form.

The angular nature of age uke does lead itself to deflecting downward strikes, but your timing must be impeccable to meet and deflect that strike without breaking your arm—remember, pushing away from you is not where you are strongest.

Take an attacker who drops a pummelling blow from on high. With body-positioning we can be out from underneath it before it comes to land. At the same time, our parrying hand—a natural reaction (the flinch reaction) trained to became a ward or parry makes that first contact from the side of (not beneath) that descending blow.

Again, it is worth noting that we do not try to resist force with force, as whoever's force is greater will win and it might not be us.

Now pulling that attacking hand down (we wouldn't want it to be used again), we thrust our right arm upwards directly under the attacker's elbow. Hitting into the golgi-body/golgi tendon and then twisting the arm (while still making contact) causes a severe release of the elbow.

When working with a partner it is important for their safety that both of you know to "tap" when there is pain.

Your aim is to achieve a tap with the least effort, not the most.

At the same time as looking for the achievement of pain in a partner, we must be aware that everyone has different pain thresholds. This makes it very difficult sometimes, as there is no correlation between the amount of effort you use and the amount of pain someone else feels. Your greatest wrench might produce very little or your smallest twist might produce howls. You must begin lightly and work up to the level that your partner is comfortable with. Everything beyond that must be left to visualisation and kata practice.

Should your partner rise onto their toes with this technique then be even more careful, especially if they haven't indicated pain yet. They are inches away from an arm break as their bodyweight will hang from their shoulder.

Respect for training partners is paramount.

Age uke

A further variation of the technique can be found when we consider the "inside" of the movement—the *ura*– rather than the surface—the *omote*—application.

Grappling situations are all too common. We have already let our guard down and allowed ourselves to be grabbed. The next stage will have us on the floor being trampled, so we have to end the confrontation.

We seek to pull the attacker in to head-butt them. Should a head-butt be your favoured technique then you probably have great ways of doing it. For those of us who do not favour head-butts, we are left with the fear of doing it and to help us cope we will use a "corner" of our head rather than risk the "mask" area.

We accelerate the damage done by cracking in to the base of the attacker's occipital lobe of the brain with our thumb-knuckle. The strike is directly towards our head, meaning that there will be impact from two directions to one central part of the brain.

If we are well trained (or lucky) we can make sure that the strikes are opposite each other in terms of the attacker's physiology as well.

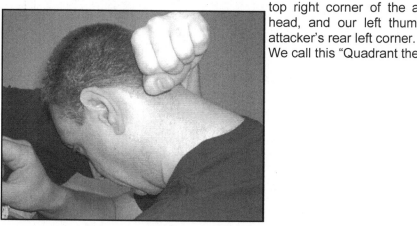

This would have, for best effect, our forehead at the top right corner of the attacker's head, and our left thumb at the attacker's rear left corner.
We call this "Quadrant theory".

Age uke

Where the attacker has grabbed us with both hands we must overcome the initial shock to be able to react at all.

Drop one hand down on their arm, preferably on the brachio radialis, to disrupt them. Angling this strike inwards across the body also turns the attacker slightly. With the attacker turned there is less likelihood of them continuing with that imminent attack.

At the same time we ram our other forearm up under their jaw with a twisting motion. You should find that the forearm lines itself up perfectly with the line of the jaw when it is twisted this way.

Remember that most of the effect is caused by the "spinning" nature of the forearm rather than the strength of the practitioner.

If training this technique with a partner, make sure that their tongue is safely in their mouth, and that their jaw is clenched or risk blood and shattered teeth.

Once more, don't neglect the application of forward moving bodyweight that is so frequently seen as "stance".

Age uke

Going through the reasons for kata existing, it might be worth considering that the kata represent an increase in the level of the threat that the practitioner faces the further into the kata—and the family of kata– that you get. The highest kata, then, would represent the most severe threats and the most severe responses. This happens on a smaller scale with each individual kata.

As the threat level is increased, we find ourselves in a clinch. Staying in close, we seize the attacker's hair from behind—rubbing the knuckles into the scalp—with one hand and pull down.

Simultaneously pushing the forearm up into their throat.

In this case we see Age uke as a neck crank with a full rotation of the attacker's head.

Either hand could be brutal enough to end the confrontation. Both together, working in different ways to accomplish the same ends is much more certain.

This differs from the application shown earlier in that we haven't struck the arm because the danger is already upon us. Instead we use the same paradigm to bring quadrant theory into the equation and used two hands to twist the head!

Turning gedan barai

You could use this technique the same way it has already been shown.

But, this is a big anticlockwise 90 degree turn. So let's give it a different possible meaning.

Once you have already struck someone, it is imperative that you put yourself in a better position to leave or incapacitate them further.

The strike could be any of the age uke applications already shown, or a punch like in *Kihon* kata.

Either way, we take the move following a *kiai* as an indication of someone who has already been struck. This means that there will be compliance, but that the threat level was high enough to warrant further restrictions on the attacker's liberty.

Taking hold of the attacker by the shoulder or the back of their neck, keep them close to you; utilising the "leave no gap" principle we will throw the attacker.

The other option is to reach all the way around and grasp the attacker's chin. Take care in practice.

Throw your body around, ensuring that a strong hip is present for them to be thrown over.

Essentially, this throw leaves the front foot (right in this illustration) where it is and rotates the back foot around to generate our spiral.

The further the turn, and the more angles that they are forced to pass through, the better your chances of getting them to the ground.

Obviously we affect balance, using our quadrant theory principle this time to throw. We've previously seen it used to strike. Now we've added another dimension to the principle.

Oi-zuki Chudan

The next punch can be taken to mean the same as previous punches.

Turning gedan barai

You could use this technique the same way it has already been shown. Or like this...

Before, we concentrated on the effect of an attacker in front of us, and how we could use the rotation in this turn to throw them behind us.

This time, we will take It that the attacker is behind us.

He could have come up behind us, or perhaps we were having words and we tried to leave the confrontation before it escalated. In this scenario, the attacker won't let us leave, so we must respond.

He grabs our shoulder to turn us into his punch.

As we were trying to leave anyway, we continue to pull forward a little, just to unbalance the attacker.

Our flinch reaction is used to turn us and cover our body from imminent harm. Usefully, this time our flinch also bars the back of the attacker's elbow. This begins to turn him (and his other weapon) away from us.

As we are now facing the attacker's "blind side", we can inject a quick BAR type of strike into his ribs, or kidneys if they present themselves.

As the striking hand travels back towards us and the covering hand begins it's outward motion, we should bring some part of the attacker back with us. In this case we have managed to attach an elbow, but it could be their coat, or hair, or...

Our outbound hand goes across the top of the attacker's arm and against his neck. Effectively, this gedan barai is now a strike with a downward course—which is precisely where we want to leave our attacker.

Oi-zuki Chudan

The next punch can be taken to mean the same as previous punches.

Turning Gedan Barai

Now, you could use the gedan barai in the same fashion as the previous times that it has been used.

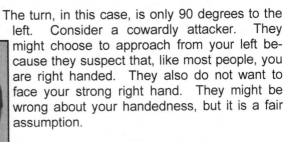

The turn, in this case, is only 90 degrees to the left. Consider a cowardly attacker. They might choose to approach from your left because they suspect that, like most people, you are right handed. They also do not want to face your strong right hand. They might be wrong about your handedness, but it is a fair assumption.

The attack is initiated by the attacker placing their hand on your shoulder. Their intention is to turn you *into* their strike, thereby both multiplying the force of their strike and reducing your chances of coping by dizzying you.

This version is the opposite side of the body to the version previously seen at the other end of the main performance line, using the opposite hands.

Now, when the attacker's left hand has grabbed you and they intend to hit you with their right, they might also intend to turn you so that they can hit the back of your head.

Witness how the kata shows an escalating level of danger as it progresses, even though the techniques look the same as ones you have already used.

Raise your elbow to cover your centreline and immediately press it against the elbow of the attacker. This short movement makes it a lot harder for them to hit you. You have barred their elbow and used the flinch reaction to cover yourself.

At the same time, reach below your own arm to grab theirs (or strike to the ribs again).

Pulling their arm towards you, your uppermost left elbow and forearm will descend sharply towards the attacker's neck and drive them to the ground.

The use of persistent, multiple strikes is necessary to take away the attacker's ability to cope. A non-aggressive person might be put off by the first jarring of their elbow by your raised elbow. At the same time, a non-aggressive person is unlikely to be attacking you. If you have caught them by surprise and they don't want to continue to attack then you don't have to continue to defend; but if they are aggressive and you need to continue, then continue vigorously, strike the ribs, strike the head, continue until it is safe to leave.

Once again, do not underestimate the use of body-weight and direction. It is the stance that gives the final blow it's direction.

Oi-zuki Chudan
The next punch can be taken to mean the same as previous punches.

Oi-zuki Chudan
The next punch can be taken to mean the same as previous punches.

Oi-zuki Chudan
The next punch can be taken to mean the same as previous punches.

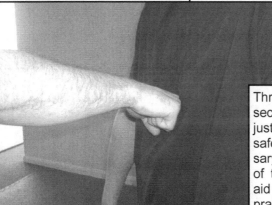

Three punches performed consecutively could mean that you just hit people a lot until you are safe. It could be that it is necessary to take you back to the start of the performance line and to aid memory, or to make you practice your punch more than some other technique.

It could just be, though, that it is an indicator that the right fist hits more over the heart side of an attacker.

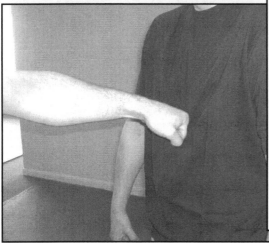

You see, punching centrally, the *seiken* fist will always lie slightly more over the heart with the right than the left.

The kata tells us to hit with the right, or the left, - but preferably the right—and it underlines this with a **kiai**.

Turning Shuto Uke

Very similar in it's principles to gedan barai. This turn has previously been used as a throw after striking. Here, we look at a different type of finish, using slightly different mechanics.

As we turn to finish the person who has assaulted us, we find it necessary to squeeze their elbow close to our chest

Instead of throwing them to the floor we have the idea that we can use leverage with our elbow while impacting with the edge of the hand (a suitable weapon for a narrow target like the neck) to increase the effectiveness.

The use of the stance in this situation reminds us that we will keep our weight back rather than throwing everything forward. This tells us that there is more in the pivot than mere strength.

We are *pulling* even though we are stepping forwards with the stance.

Principle

An Open Hand is an Elbow. Whereas the closed fist drawn to your side signifies a wrist that has been grabbed, the open hand identifies that you have an opponent's elbow. The evidence is that if you place an opponent's wrist at your hip their elbow will usually end up in front of your solar plexus. The different hand position shows how much harder it is to close your grasp around an elbow and also the idea of trapping the forearm with your own. The open hand does not rely upon a grip with the fingers to be effective.

Shuto uke

In this variation, the attacker has placed a hand on us ready to strike.

This hand quite often takes the form of a push, and is used subconsciously by the attacker to test you. They are trying to upset your equilibrium by putting BAR into you, and at the same time they get to see what kind of resistance you will offer before the fight is "on".

We use the flinch reaction cover the centre-line. Should our hand happen to flash in front of the attacker's eyes and disorient him, then this will prove useful, too.

Simultaneously, we inject the fingertips into the supra-sternal notch of the attacker. The gag reflex that this causes makes it hard for the attacker to continue, setting up the rest of the technique.

The arm that draws across the body might have some small impact on the brachio radialis of the attacker, folding their arm across their body. If we fear that we cannot accomplish this with subtlety then we should crash the elbow down on the attacker's elbow instead.

The jerking of their neck and turning of their body provides exactly the right angle to deliver a chop across the carotid sinus and sternocleido mastoid.

Great care must be taken in practice, as this strike has been known to provide knock outs. If you are not in control of your partner's bodyweight then dropping them may damage their skull on the floor, and that could prove fatal.

It is important to know that the technique will harm people, to be better equipped in your decision to use it. WE hope to never encounter a situation where such force was necessary, and, knowing the ramifications, we are better able to NOT use the technique when the situation does not warrant it.

Stepping 45 degree shuto uke

Should the single impact not have the desired effect, a following shot at 45 degrees will conform to our quadrant theory principles by striking upwards against the back of the head whilst the previous chop struck down against the opposite side of the neck.

Note that although the grip is changed from one hand to the other, we do not let go of the attacker's limb once it has been seized. This idea of sticking to them is very useful.

In practice be careful of the whiplash your partner feels from being chopped first on one side and then being jerked so that you can access the other side of their neck.

Turning Shuto uke

Taking another look at the "hand on the shoulder" routine.

Turning to the outside line of our would-be assailant, we are once again going to try to access their "blind side".

This time we find that our flinch has gone too high to effect the arm-bar that we are so fond of.

We bring our elbow down on top of the attacker's arm, drawing them in.

Throughout this portion of the movement we are covered against any continuation of the attack. Don't forget that if further BAR is necessary then we must not overlook it just because it doesn't appear to be covered by the kata.

It is entirely possible that the attacker will involuntarily launch his head forward from your pull so vigorously that he will head-butt your elbow. Take care in practice.

Alternative view

Stepping into the attacker, we keep our bodyweight back, so that they are pulled towards us.

Our elbow is brought crashing down into the attacker's shoulder, causing pain and damage and further unbalancing them.

We chop directly across their neck, effecting the airway and the blood passageways.

In practice, we have often seen the attacker fall before the chop gets anywhere near their neck, purely from the displacement of their balance by the strike with the elbow and the subsequent direction from the arm. Should this occur you should not be unduly concerned. It only means that you have been prevented from dealing a harmful blow by the attacker's lack of resistance.

In effect, they have taken themselves out of the fight.

45 degree Shuto uke

The attacker has grabbed the lapel to draw you on to his fist.

Our hands are up. We do not stand around in a "yoi" position on the street.

One of the surest ways for us to gauge the situation and to subconsciously limit the attack is to bring our hands up to talk to them.

Geoff Thompson makes much of this in his works on "*The Fence*", and readers are encouraged to familiarise themselves with all of his work.

Suffice to say, our subliminal guard is about to be by-passed, so we will have to take action.

The attacker's hand is already upon us, so we make use of it by cutting across the wrist with our wrist. We use the nearest hand to do so, as it is less obvious in it's intentions.

This one factor is going to disrupt the attacker's intention and his balance.

To take a 45 degree step forwards:

The elbow can be used either against the back of the attacker's arm (triceps tendon), or brought down on top of the attacker's elbow again.

By stepping out at 45 degrees and adhering to the attacker with the other arm (from an "outside line") we can easily strike the delicate area below the occipital lobe of the brain, harming short term memory and eyesight.

Again, in practice, care must be taken. We suggest that after any light strike to the head you ask your partner to gauge the impact on a scale of 1-10, with1 being no effect and 10 being "I'm going to pass out". On an upward scale we suggest that you don't train above your partner's level 6 or 7. This shouldn't be attempted at all without a qualified instructor.

Remember, even if your partner says "4" if their eyes are glassy or they wobble on their heels do not practice any further.

Yame Withdraw to mark the end of this kata. Don't forget to remain alert, as it could all begin again at any second.

Heian Nidan

平安二段

HEIAN NIDAN

Peaceful Mind Level Two

This used to be the first Heian kata, but Master Funakoshi considered it too difficult for raw beginners.

Of note in this kata are the introduction of gyaku techniques and morote uke, and that the second kiai does not occur on the main embusen, but rather on the final technique.

This is the first kata in the family to have a stance transition in stepping forwards instead of turning.

From a ready position.

Sink the weight and look to the left. Step out into back stance whilst throwing the arms up so that the left forearm is vertical with the palm of the fist forwards and 90° to the upper arm. The right arm should make a position similar to a horizontal age uke. The right middle knuckle is on the same horizontal plane as the left wrist.

Corkscrew the right fist to throat height whilst withdrawing the left fist back to the right ear. The elbows are tucked in and the stance does not change, though the body angle is to the left and the body is contracted.

Expand the chest and left arm to make a horizontal hammerfist whilst the right fist makes hikite.

Look to the right, lower the arms, and pivot on the heels to face the right in backstance. Throw the arms up so that they mirror the position for the first technique.

Corkscrew the left fist to the throat whilst withdrawing the right fist back to the left ear. The elbows are tucked in and the stance does not change. Contract the body and angle to the right.

Expand the chest and right arm to make a horizontal hammerfist whilst the left fist makes hikite.

Black Belt Tip: Don't change height here. Coil and release.

Look directly behind, over the right shoulder. Pull the left foot half-way towards the right and change the direction to face the right whilst pulling the right vertical fist to the left horizontal fist. Momentarily right sits on top of left.

Pull the right foot back and kick yoko keage to the rear, simultaneously making right vertical fist uraken. The intention is to place the foot and fist at the same place. As the foot and fist snap back, turn to the front and cross the arms in preparation for making shuto uke along the main embusen.

Step down into left kokutsudachi and make shuto uke.
Step forward into right kokutsudachi and make shuto uke.
Step forward into left kokutsu dachi and make shuto uke.
Drop the left hand to the horizontal position, step forward into zenkutsudachi and thrust the right hand forwards, nukite. The fingers of the left hand should rest fractionally behind the right elbow, palm down. **Kiai**.

Look to the right. Pull the left hip sharply and turn 90° anti-clockwise to make left kokutsudachi and shuto uke to the right.
Look to the right. Step out at 45° into right kokutsudachi and make shuto uke.
Look over the right shoulder. Pull the right hip sharply back and turn 135° clockwise, then step out to the left, making right kokutsudachi and shuto uke,
Step out at 45° into left kokutsudachi and make shuto uke.

Alternate view

Alternate view

Push the left foot onto the main embusen and make zenkutsudachi.

As the body pushes past shomen the right hand slides under the left arm and then out to make gyaku uchi uke. The left hand makes hikite. The chest is aimed at contra 45° or reverse hanmi, coiling the hip.

Black Belt Tip: Coiling the hip makes the front foot retract slightly. If this is not done then either the stance was too short initially or the front knee has straightened, neither of which are advisable.

Kick maegeri with the right leg, and punch gyakuzuki as the foot steps forward into right zenkutsudachi.

Black Belt Tip: Time the foot landing from the kick with fist going out. "Foot and fist together".

Without changing the stance, make left gyaku uchi uke, coiling the left hip into reverse hanmi. As this happens, the right foot may well move as the hip is pulled back. This is *not* a step, but an indicator of correct hip rotation.

Kick maegeri with the left leg, and punch gyakuzuki as the foot steps forward into left zenkutsudachi.

Step forward into right zenkutsudachi. As the body catches up with the forward fist, cross the wrists and roll them first across the body to the left hip, and then forwards to make morote uke. The knuckle of the left little finger should touch the inside of the right forearm.

Look to the right. Pull the left hip sharply up and turn 90° anti-clockwise, preparing the arms for gedan barai. Step out to the right into left zenkutsudachi and make gedan barai.

Look to the right. Step out at 45° into right zenkutsudachi and make age uke.

Black Belt Tip: Don't forget that gedan barai and age uke are two handed manoeuvres and so a "middle position must be made between the moves.

Look to the right. Pull the right hip sharply back, turning 135° clockwise and step out into right zenkutsu dachi, making gedan barai.

Look to the left. Step out at 45° into left zenkutsudachi and make age uke. **Kiai**.

Yamae.
Naore.

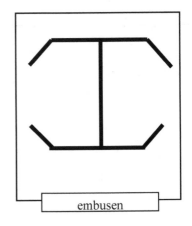

embusen

Applications

Let's consider that this used to be the first kata in the series, as created by Master Itosu. Master Funakoshi is said to have changed the order of the kata for ease of learning. This would not change the priorities of the techniques.

The first kata must deal with the most likely situations—the beginning of the conflict. Whereas the current Heian Shodan kata begins with someone having already grabbed your lapels, this form begins with that "tester" of spirit and inducer of the flight-or-fight syndrome the Shove.

The shove represents any hand that comes directly towards you. It could just as easily be a straight jab to the chin. It's just that jabs are not as common as hook punches.

As the hand comes towards you, the natural flinch reflex will see you on "the back-foot" and throwing your hands up in front of you. This becomes a trained

Principle
Adaptability. Whatever techniques make up your arsenal must be useful for more than one situation.

Principle
Cross-body motor reaction. Pulling on one side of the body has an equal and opposite reaction upon the other side of the body. We can use this to our advantage by causing the Pre-Determined Response that negates any instant further attack.

technique when it is enhanced to brush aside the incoming attack rather than resisting it. The pushing hand is latched onto, and the other raised arm is brought into contact with the attackers elbow, momentarily disrupting any attempt to "lock up".

Resist all thoughts that either hand is merely a "ready" hand, about to be used. Hands don't have to be put into preposterous positions to be "ready".

Pull the attacker's arm into you with your leading arm while pushing their wrist back along the path it came, set/lock the wrist.

In practice, we tend to only take the wrist through two angles. It is apparent that a third angle, as shown in performing the kata, will break the wrist.

Snap the wrist towards your hip, then thrust your arm across their throat.

In practice we allow the wrist out away from our body, to prevent injury to our partner. This goes against our "leave no gap" principle, which can be seen to break the wrist if adhered to.

Principle
Base. All joint locks need a base or they will fail.

An alternative application, which we can show as the display by the other side of the body, again involves that initial part of the confrontation.

In this case, our words have failed us and we have no where left to run, so we are left to deal with the incoming assault.

Against the common right hook, we throw our arms up to prevent the impact, while letting the attacker's bodyweight deliver their face onto our waiting right forearm.

There is a beneficial effect in striking "up" the face instead of all at once. Try to make contact with the lower end of the forearm first.

This turns their face away from us; reducing the likelihood of them throwing their other fist.

It is obvious that this is another trained version of the "flinch" reaction. Taking a natural impulse and converting it into a defensive paradigm.

Remember that as all applications take place part of the way through the movement, the forearm slammed into the attacker's face should not just stop, but rather continue through.

Take hold of the attacker's turned face and pull his head back towards your shoulder. Push their punching arm through the gap to close it down and make the attacker face completely away from you.

The facility to sit your weight backwards helps to absorb the incoming punch and continue the attacker's momentum through the circle so that they face away from you without getting the chance to throw their left fist.

Those who wish to control the individual instead of harming him might wish to use this posture to effect a "face bar" across the eyebrow, thereby buying compliance.

Those who whish to strike now use their forearm or hammer-fist directly.

The out-going strike is now across the back of the neck.

Of course, if you wished to hold on to the hair this would make a nasty wrench of the neck.

In practice we tend to let go of the attacker and allow them to roll out of this movement, again, for their safety.

Koshi-gamae

This "preparatory position" is used to bring an opponent in.

You need to ensnare them, whether by working against a cross-arm grab or by getting to the outside of a punch and taking hold of the punching arm.

The attacker's wrist is pulled to the hip and turned over—this means that their elbow is facing upwards.

You place your elbow against their elbow which prevents them from rising and then set their wrist at right-angles to their forearm. Should the attacker show any resistance, the smallest of taps on their upturned elbow with your elbow brings them back into compliance.

The whole technique is performed with a heavy, sticky feeling, so that even when you change grips you never let go of the attacker completely.

Don't rely on this situation holding the attacker forever, though. Any pain can be quickly controlled, so it is imperative to move on to another method of dealing with them immediately.

> **Principle**
> **Variable Pain**. When any lock is placed, vary the intensity to keep it viable. Constant pain can be resisted.

Uraken & Yoko keage

Following on form the last technique, with the attacker under your control momentarily. Should it be necessary to continue working on them to prevent further threat to yourself or your family:

The first part of a kick is to raise your knee, which impacts into the attacker's ribs. Reasonably formidable on its own, this technique is best served as a dose of BAR to buy compliance.

Your foot is then thrown upwards to strike into the attacker's leg. Which leg it hits is of little consequence, and you can find one without looking down just by performing the kick.

The crescent of your kick has an adverse effect on the knee. The rising nature of the kick brings the head slightly more upwards, ready to be struck.

Release the wrist to strike the attacker's temple with your back-fist. Again, working on the principle of "feel your way", if you run your arm along their arm, you find their head without the need to look for it directly.

The strike also turns the attacker's face away from you; helping to prevent any further attacks.

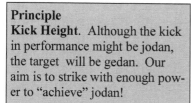

Principle
Kick Height. Although the kick in performance might be jodan, the target will be gedan. Our aim is to strike with enough power to "achieve" jodan!

Shuto uke

As previously seen, we use shuto to chop the attacker's neck.

In this example we use the shuto as the most severe neck twist. It follows on directly from the previous technique.

By passing the arms either side of the head we twist the neck in one direction without the use of fine motor skills.

The outgoing motion of shuto uke is used to propel the head; rotating in the opposite direction to the "ready position".

Should the bodyweight be added to the technique by dropping back down into a back stance having already disrupted the opponent's balance with the side kick to the knee, then we find that virtually their full weight is hanging from their neck.

Note, once again, that the "action" occurs in the middle of the movement.

In this kata we are advised that his technique can be done with your left hand or your right hand, but that if you use your left hand you might like to follow it with another technique. In this kata we are advised to use nukite.

> **Principle**
> **Space Between**. Although in performance the arms touch, that doesn't mean you can't place something (like a head) between them.

Shuto uke

In this application, we take the position that the attacker has thrust a jab towards our face.

We seek to access the blind-side by shifting the body to the outside line position.

Bringing our arm over the top of the attacker's arm, we retain it by pinching it to our body without trying to grab with our fingers.

At the same time our other arm is still up high having deflected the blow, and as it passes across the top of the attacker's arm we may well find that their head shoots forwards onto our waiting elbow.

That same elbow then drops down into the attacker's shoulder. The preferable location is the joining of the *deltoid* with the *pectoralis minoris*.

Our forearm is delivered as a narrow weapon across the throat. Note that the whole arm is used, not just the hand.

Note that the use of bodyweight into a back stance leaves the front foot as a device to trip the attacker as he is pushed back by our chop. Think of it as a base or a bridge.

Nukite

The "spear hand" technique is preceded by a short *osae uke*—pressing block.

This often over-looked part of the technique makes primary sense of the application.

When thrusting with the fingertips we must be very careful which part of the attacker we impact on, as the fingertips are not as strong as, say, your knuckles.

When we impact on the attacker's forearms (preferably with a cutting motion rather than a slapping one) we bring them down so that their throat is directly in front of our middle level. Keeping their arms in place, we can drive our fingertips directly forwards into their throat just below the adam's apple and above the suprasternal notch.

This provides us with a "gag relex" that is a suitable inhibitor of the attacker's aggression.

To follow on from this position would be similar to following on from the punch (with kiai) point in Heian Shodan.

The set of four Shuto uke can be used as shown previously in the Heian Shodan section.

Side View

Gyaku-uchi uke, maegeri, gyakuzuki

The jab is thrown and we use our flinch reaction to drive us to the side, covering our head as we do so.

Once we have evaded the attacker's punch we must deal directly with the limb that has been given to us.

Sticking to the limb, the attacker's hand is pulled down to our hip and their balance so disturbed.

If at all possible, the attacker's arm should be rotated as it is pulled, but don't concentrate on this to the detriment of the direction of the movement.

We use the opportunity to strike against the back of their elbow, cutting into and against the golgi-body/tendon. This motion snakes around the arm without losing contact, pinching nerves against bones before the impact of the uchi uke.

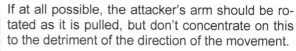

> **Principle**
> **Front=Down, Back=Up.** When we make contact with an opponent, if the contact is to the front of the body there should be a downward angle on it. Contact to the back of the body should have an upward angle to it for maximum disruption.

Swiftly raising our knee, we make impact into whatever part of their anatomy presents itself. This is rarely the groin. The attacker will be twisted in their orientation in relation to you, so that their side will be available as a target. This is the purpose of the uchi uke technique.

Alternatively, deep impact into the thigh can cause a temporary paralysis of the limb, and deep damage to large muscles is always harder to fix than damage to small muscles.

We can also usually reach the ribs with the knee, so there are a variety of targets.

Our foot is thrust forward forcefully. It will usually catch the inside of one of the attacker's knees.

Impacting on the inside of the knee is very dangerous, as it is mechanically not built to withstand sideways (or shear) pressure.

We are fond of warning that this is a life-changing technique, and so must not be used needlessly.

You don't have to look down to make this happen, the close proximity will do the job.

As your bodyweight is driven forwards, your hand continues to pull on the attacker's arm, combined with the kick in the knee they will turn around so that their back is open to you.

Gyakuzuki, connecting half-way through it's motion, looks just like an upper-cut punch, and this one connects at the kidneys. You do, of course, continue *through* the target until you make full extension of the technique.

What we observe here is that the full technique takes us from the upper right quadrant to the lower left quadrant and then to the rear of the upper right quadrant, flowing from one to the next to get the job done.

Alternative view

Morote uke

Many of the applications that we see can be used as joint locks of one description or another. No amount of twisting of wrists can be beaten by a simple collision on an anatomically vulnerable area.

When the upper arm has been seized it presents us with a valuable opportunity to strike into the *brachio radialis* muscle that lies just below the elbow.

The reaction from this strike brings the attacker's head forwards at a speed that you cannot control. By thrusting forward with your body-weight at the same time you present your other fist for their throat or jaw to slam into.

In practice we take care to ensure that the attacker's head comes forward before the striking fist is produced. In order to train our minds and bodies to produce the right results under pressure, we must use visualisation and kata practice to teach us to use both hands simultaneously.

Turning gedan barai

It seems most natural then, once an impact of this sort has been delivered, to step around and throw the other party to the floor.

We have seen this turn in Kihon kata and Heian Shodan.

This performance of the technique is no different, except for the strike that begins the movement.

The reason for including the same application here is to show that when it doesn't quite happen the way we would like it to—when we have been unsuccessful in flooring the opponent—there are further options.

So far, our options have included punching the attacker, and chopping the attacker as we follow them on their turn.

This time we will utilise our downward motion to set up an equal or greater rising motion—thereby amplifying the latter movement.

Age uke

Now, even though this technique has featured in the Heian Shodan kata, we are made aware of it here at a 45 degree angle. Please take the time to re-analyse the applications shown in the other kata and apply the body position to them. You will find that the jaw alignment is much more appropriate when this angle is added.

When the kata were first arranged, this information was passed on before the idea of using the technique in a linear fashion. It was considered more basic; more fundamental, that the 45 degree information be imparted than the student know different uses for the technique.

Although the kiai that is customary today is a fairly recent innovation, it is not much younger than these kata themselves. It is important that the kiai is placed on what some consider to be a *blocking* technique—it reveals that this last move; this final burst of energy—is enough to finish the opponent. A technique that just stopped a punch would not warrant that level of attention.

The masters have ended a kata with what some might call a block. If that were so then would still be vulnerable.

Yame. Rather than "finish", think of "return to the beginning".

Heian Sandan

平安三段

HEIAN SANDAN

Peaceful mind level three.

This kata is the first to feature a move performed slowly. Slow moves must be executed with balance and precision. They allow the practitioner a moment of recovery during kata practice and a return to the focusing of attention.

One should not become confused into thinking that the application to the technique is performed slowly.

Black Belt Tip:
The "double block" should be very fast in performance, and move fluidly from the first to the second time. Pause before turning to make uchi uke.

From a ready position.

Look to the left and prepare the arms to step out to the left into back stance and make uchi uke.

Pull the right foot to the left foot and adopt a shomen body position to the side without raising your height. Push your right arm out to a gedan barai position, then make uchi uke and gedan barai at the same time. Ensure that the elbows meet and that the characteristic tearing motion is made.

Make uchi uke and gedan barai with the opposite arms. Look over your right shoulder. Pivot 180° clockwise on your left heel and prepare the arms to make uchi uke.

Step out into back stance and make uchi uke.

Pull your left foot up to your right without raising your height and push your left fist to a gedan barai position. The body should be shomen facing to the right.

Make uchi uke and gedan barai at the same time. Ensure that the elbows meet and that the characteristic tearing motion is made.

Make gedan barai and uchi uke with the opposite arms. Look to the centre line.

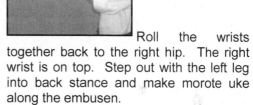

Roll the wrists together back to the right hip. The right wrist is on top. Step out with the left leg into back stance and make morote uke along the embusen.

Drop the left hand down into osae uke and step forward into front stance making nukite. The fingers of the left hand rest just behind the underside of the elbow. The hand is flat with the fingers pointed to the right.

Turn the right hand 180° counter-clockwise on a horizontal axis, then pivot 180° counter-clockwise on the right foot to land in kiba dachi.

Black Belt Tip: The osae uke is a key, but oft neglected part of the technique. Be deliberate with this move and the turn of the hand.

Pull the right fist back to hikite and make a horizontal hammerfist with the left hand. The attention is still to the front/the end of the main line.

Pivot the left heel to change the direction of the body and step forwards into front stance and make oi-zuki. **KIAI**.

Slowly, pull the left foot up to the right, simultaneously pivoting on the right heel to bring the feet together facing back down the embusen. The arms come to rest with the elbows out and the two fore-knuckles of ech hand resting on the hips. A slow "winding-up" should be felt, with the pulling motion of the hips being similar to the turn at the end of the embusen of all previous kata.

Raise the right knee up high, pivot on the left foot to bring the right foot down fumikomi forwards into kiba dachi. The right elbow swings across past the body, and then arcs to make uraken uchi descending to the bridge of the nose. The hand then returns to the hip.

Black Belt Tip: By making your knees pass close to each other you ensure that the move is fumikomi and not mikazukigeri. Be deliberate with the elbow movement to ensure that it is passed on correctly.

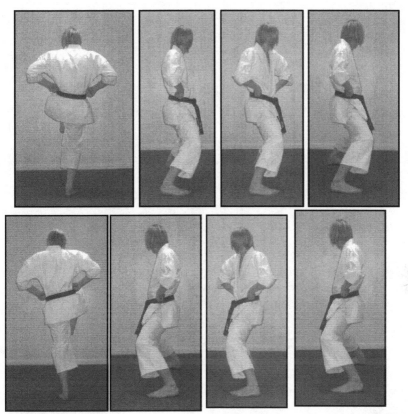

Pull the left knee up to the front, making the body shomen as you do so, then make fumikomi forwards into kiba dachi. The left elbow swings across past the body, and then the fist arcs upwards to make uraken uchi descending to the height of the bridge of the nose. The hand then returns to the hip.

Pull the right knee up to the front, making the body shomen as you do so, then make fumikomi forwards into kiba dachi. The right elbow swings across past the body, and then the fist arcs to make uraken uchi descending to the height of the bridge of the nose. The hand then returns to the hip.

Change the body's direction by pivoting on the heels towards the end of the embusen, making tate shuto as you do...

...then step forwards into zenkutsudachi and make oi-zuki chudan.

Pull the right foot up parrallel to the left, look right ...
then pivot 180° counter-clockwise on the right foot to make kiba dachi.

Black Belt Tip: By bringing the back foot up you effectively allow the same kind of turn as you had in the previous Heian kata. As before, do not change height as you do this move.

The right fist crosses the body and ends up over the left shoulder while the left hand pulls back into a tight hikite position, as though attacking with empi behind you.

The right elbow must not be higher than the bottom lip.

A subtle shift is created by throwing the bodyweight into the next move. There is no jump in this kata. Drive the left fist across the body and over the right shoulder, and make the right arm return to a tight hikite position, as though attacking with empi behind you. **KIAI.** The left elbow must not be higher than the bottom lip.

Yame.

Black Belt Tip: This "yame" requires the movement of only the right foot. To ensure neatness, have the foot draw *all* the way back to the left foot before resuming the "shizentai" position.

embusen

Applications

The growth of the student continues with the complexity of the kata. This kata, the third in the series, reveals three different stances in one sequence, suggesting a change in the way you use your bodyweight while working on someone.

Bodyweight is also important when you consider that this is the first kata to feature a deliberate change in height while performing the moves. It occurs three times over two different techniques. Twice with the "double-fast" moves and once after the first kiai.

Heian Sandan also features the first use of the infamous "slow move". This could be a method of providing drama in your performance—of catching your breath before you move again. It could also signify that you are supposed to look carefully at this particular move. Slowly means that the movement is either deadly or difficult to perform (usually both).

This intermediary level of experience is difficult for practitioners. The kata is quite short, and aside from a few subtleties, is quite easy to learn. Just like the Tekki series that follow the Heian kata, this can be deceptive.

We suggest that high grade students re-examine Heian Sandan as something of a lost treasure.

Uchi uke

Once again, we have an attacker who is about to strike us.

He has reached out and grabbed with his left hand, attaching at the lapel or collar.

In this case, we have left our guard wide enough for the attacker to reach between our hands. He's got us right where we want him!

We keep our bodyweight back and away from the opponent, turning slightly sideways for two reasons
i) to minimise the amount of target available to the attacker;
ii) to provide extra torque for the technique that we are about to use.

Our left hand adheres to the attacker's left wrist, using a monkey grip that does not involve the use of the opposable thumb on purpose.

This, then, pulls back and turns the attacker's punch away by cross-body motor reaction. *Hikite* takes us off-line.

At the same time we inject our right fist through the attacker's left elbow, catching it painfully just above the joint in the soft tissue.

The fist continues under the attacker's arm and then circle's abruptly back outwards to conclude our *uchi uke*.

> **Principle**
> **Monkey Grip**. The fingers wrap around, and if the thumb "happens" to engage then that's fine, but we don't deliberately attempt to engage the thumb. This grip should not involve conscious thought or fine motor skills. As such, we should be able to use it even under stressful conditions.

 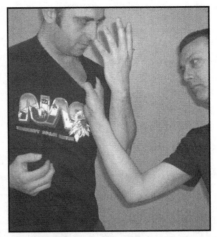

 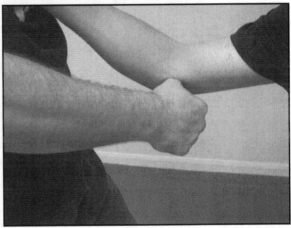

Awase uke

The attacker has grabbed ferociously. We pull our hand over the top of their arm to distract them, and at the same time squeeze it back towards us so that the attacker's elbow redirects their body and their attacking limb away from us.

In a similar function to the previous technique, we use our thumb knuckle to inject into the attacker's elbow.

Their arm has been hit in two different directions in quick succession.

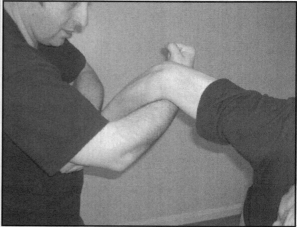

Continuing on the same path, we now take the injecting thumb around in a small circle to make *uchi uke* while our other arm grinds down to make *gedan barai* through the attacker's limb.

For restraint purposes we can slide the attacker into the position known as "hammer lock". It has his fist with the thumb facing down locked into our elbow with the thumb facing up. His weakness is caused by his arm being behind his back and upside down whilst ours is the right way up and in the power zone in front of our heart.

Potentially, we could continue the motion (as the kata instructs) by drawing those circles again and tearing through the attacker's arm. Our aim would be to tear it off, in the sure knowledge that even with a remarkably high failure rate we would still do the attacker some damage.

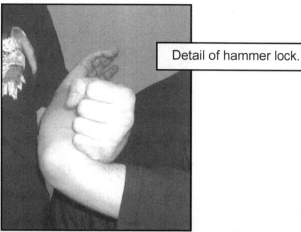

Detail of hammer lock.

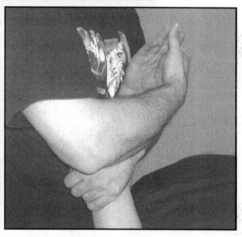

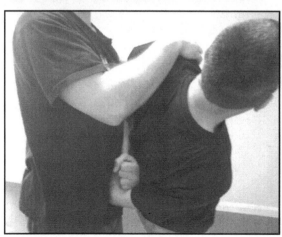

Potentially, we could "set" the wrist to help maintain compliance during this movement.

Alternatively, we enjoy a lot of success with reaching over the attacker's shoulder and gouging into the deltoid/pectoralis minoris meeting point with a strong grip.

Uchi uke

A further use for uchi uke can be found when we are attacked with a heavy right hook.

We can move in and cover the attacker's limb, then, before he can strike again, pull it sharply towards us.

Those who have studied the "soft block" know that we do not need to be strong to cover the incoming punch. The audacity to interrupt the attacker's impetus is required, but any strength/tension in your arm or shoulder leads to it buckling under a heavy blow.

Pulling the attacker in towards you reveals the target for your strike and it also causes whiplash.

Our other arm folds out and strikes with the heavier of the two bones—the radius—into the attacker's neck. The rolling motion of uchi uke cuts down and into the attacker's body with the force of the blow.

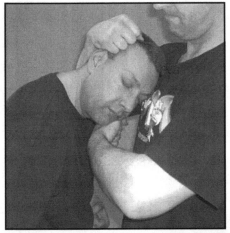

A further application could follow from just about any situation.

Take any time we have been dragged in close and had to administer a BAR strike.

The entry technique could have been dealing with a grab; it could have been a punch; it could have been a shove; you understand that the range and intensity that will come from someone performing one of the habitual acts of physical violence is quite different from a kumite move.

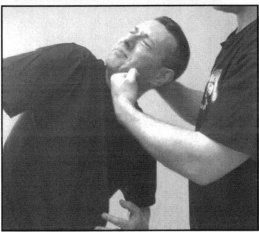

If the situation warranted it, there might be appropriate cause to take hold of the back of the attacker's head and to place the thumb knuckle at the opposite corner of the jaw.

The violence of this action is to reverse the hand positions sharply.

Never complete this move in practice.

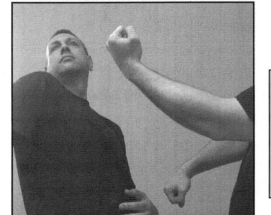

Principle
Height Change. Standing up and moving forward takes our weight in a whole new direction. See how dropping or pushing or pulling would not have the same effect.

Morote uke

The attacker has grabbed our wrist, working across the body.

We turn that wrist over in a small circle to send the attacker away, and at the same time hit into the brachio radialis to pull them back towards us. This two-way action folds the body and the arm into something like a centre -lock.

The sliding motion of our free hand is out towards the attacker's face, which he gladly presents for us to hit!

Again, the violence of this movement makes controlling the attacker's forward speed very difficult. Delay the strike when working with a partner, as even a headguard won't stop him from being knocked out if he slams his jaw into your fist.

The reason for the practice of *solo* kata should become more and more apparent as we progress with our training.

Otoshi uke, nukite

Often neglected by those studying kata, the *otoshi uke* movement provides the key to understanding the *nukite* that follows it.

Our flinch reaction to an incoming punch has been trained to guard us and take our body outside the line of the attack.

The pressing motion of the otoshi uke/osae uke is shown to steer the attacker away from you and pull them down. They present their throat in front of you, similar to the previous use of nukite in Heian Nidan.

Now, however, we are located much more strategically off to the side— a much safer location for us. Jabbing the fingers directly into the throat isn't easy from here, so we make sure that we use the fingers and palm as a guide for *our thumb* to move the windpipe laterally.

The anatomy of the windpipe means that there is some room for it to be moved backwards, but very little side-to-side movement is possible without breaking it.

Again, be careful in practice as emergency surgery is necessary to correct the broken cartilage should you use full intent.

Principle
Not Necessarily the most **Obvious Weapon.**

Turning Tettsui uchi

As the situation progresses, it is natural for us to turn our hand over in order to ensnare the attacker's neck while still pulling them down.

There are other ways that we can ensnare the neck, but many of them involve pushing the opponent back upright as you reach around the front of their throat.

As your arm stays in contact with the attacker's neck it is easy to slide your thumb edge under the jaw.

Your own hand is then locked into you by placing the hand by your own kidney. If you try to just hang on to the attacker they will be able to pull their head out of the hole; but if their jaw is locked into one side of the hole and their shoulder is on the other side then they cannot pull out.

For the sake of our partner, we often train this move upright. When we look at the kata and the continuing turn you will notice the use of horse-riding stance.

Principle:
See how the changes in stance are used to change from pulling to pushing to dropping the opponent. See how they **Link.**

The "seated" position of the stance drops the bodyweight down, and effectively provides a leg and hip for the attacker to fall over.

If you maintain the grab on the attacker's head as you turn, then their bodyweight hangs from their neck as they fall.

Oi-zuki chudan

Looking at the failure rate of the technique; if you have managed to turn but they did not fall, then you always have the option of completely changing your tactics and just forging ahead with a fist strike into the attacker's throat.

"The Slow move"

In the next sequence we have a subtle variation on the previous sequence.

Having struck the attacker we buy some compliance. It gives us the time to wrap their neck into the grab. A further variation might be if they attempted to tackle us to the ground by our waist. Having splayed the feet to prevent their driving us back we can then adapt this sequence.

Seizing the attacker's available arm to prevent it striking us, we hook into the throat. The variation on the last sequence is that we now stand upright.

The major advantage of not being tall is that by tilting our own pelvis forward we put more strain on the attacker's neck.

Resist the temptation to go up onto your toes to raise the attacker—this is contrary to what you really want. Your own pelvis must start the movement below the level of the attacker's pelvis in order for leverage to be on our side.

Principle
Look Carefully at **Slow Moves**. They represent something to do with the lethality of the technique or the difficulty of applying it, and usually both.

Hiza geri, empi uke, uraken

The point of raising your knee for any move is usually to knee the opponent. This sequence has arranged that for us beautifully.

Whether you contact the groin, the gut, or even up into the sternum with your knee, we continue immediately by driving our foot down through the attacker's knee.

Once again this causes them to have their whole bodyweight hanging form their neck, which is safely tucked under your arm.

If we continue as before, then we drop the opponent's bodyweight over our hip by dropping our bodyweight into the familiar *kiba dachi*.

Should the situation warrant it, we might find it appropriate to keep hold of the attacker's jaw while pulling the hand out from our hip, spinning in a vertical arc.

This "inside" version of the technique—the ura rather than the omote—is the last straw in a dire situation.

Remember that just because the move is in the kata it does not mean that any master has given permission for it to be used. The law simply cannot condone this kind of application conducted deliberately.

For education purposes, then, we might study the methods and manner that an Okinawan dignitary might have had to fall back on. Many people today re-enact historical situations without themselves being accused of barbarism.

We must be careful that martial artists know the law. We must also be careful that old methods do not fall into obscurity and that the kata we pass on have valid applications.

Throughout this book, it is true that just because an application exists that doesn't give you permission to use it. Great care must be taken in practice, and much like sword kata, we do not go around trying the moves on anyone.

A minor variation provides us with an alternative piece of bunkai.

In this situation, we have not managed to ensnare the attacker with him facing the rear, but rather he faces the same way we do.

Again, we have overbalanced him and put a snare around his neck.

Again we have taken hold of his available arm to prevent it's use.

The major difference is that this time he will fall over our hip head first. In the last version we could allow the attacker to fall gently if we so wished. Now, controlling that descent is much harder to do, as his own bodyweight will accelerate that fall (arriving, as it does, after the head).

Taking a further variation on the theme, we can look at a standing grapple situation.

Make note that we arrange for the situation to develop by using our knowledge of the attacker's joints to manipulate their balance.

Just because the kata is performed in a direct line forwards does not mean that there will not be some jostling for position before the event actually gets to where we want it to be.

Pull on the elbows, push on the shoulders, prod or slap down into the hips if you have to.

Don't overlook the distractions available by spitting, yelling, or even just blowing on the attacker's face before you own the situation enough to conduct a potentially dangerous throw.

Remember that all throws involve you being off balance. Your job is to make sure that the attacker is more off-balance than you are before you move in.

The set begins with kneeing the attacker. Again, groin, chest, leg, gut. We knee them wherever we can get.

Here, we manipulate the balance so far as to throw the attacker to the floor, once again using our hip and kiba dachi as our base.

With the wrists still in our grasp, we can arrange ourselves outside of the attacker's real potential kicking area.

All of this must happen quickly so that he situation does not develop into a ground-grappling situation. So, as we sit, we turn the attacker's wrists over so that the back of their elbows lies across our knees. The pressure that we bring to bear with our weight on the attacker's wrists effects their elbows and you can watch your training partner arc their back to try to relieve the stress you place on their joints.

This, of course, can buy us another few precious moments to get to where we want to be.

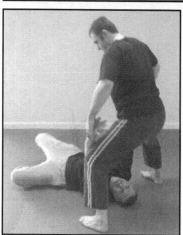

Take one of the arm-bars that you have applied and force it further to cause the attacker to roll over.

With the attacker's face ground into the floor we could use the same technique in reverse—you just have to re-obtain the other arm. Then you can force their elbows against your knees again.

A small reference to old-time wrestling sees us taking the attacker's prone form by the legs and hoisting them so that the attacker's face is still in towards the floor.

The more we utilise the stance and sit downwards the worse it is for the attacker.

The more we can tilt the pelvis without actually overbalancing, the worse it is for the attacker.

Without overly concentrating on the threatening hand, we watch for the incoming punch.

Before that punch can reach it's optimum velocity, we inject the edge of the hand into the meeting of the bicep and deltoid, or directly into the bicep.

The attacker's strength is added to the weight of our blow, and the stun that this causes gives us the time to enter the situation properly with a direct driving punch. We take a hard weapon (our fist) to a soft target (their throat).

Note that once we have intercepted the attacker's fist we maintain contact with that arm, using it to pull them on to our fist.

Once we have begun our retaliations, we must not stop until we have concluded the job. That might be when we can run. It might be that the situation will not be concluded without the apprehension of the assailant. It might be that you have to go further.

We choose to step up and enter the attacker's zone of control, but only because we are sure that they no longer have that control. The reason for this is to "leave no gap" for them when we begin our throw.

We slip our right hand to their right elbow and seize the attacker's throat with our left hand (thumb down).

Moving them over our hip, we intend to place our hands as they are in the kata. The attacker's weight might dictate otherwise, but it allows for a failure rate in the delivery. If you succeed then great, and if you only get halfway you still achieve a throw.

A variation is available by grabbing all the way around the attacker's neck from behind (if the size of them allows it).

Far from striking someone over your shoulder when they try to achieve a bear-hug, the fist is actually preventive of a choke.

By rights, you should be aware of your surroundings enough to prevent someone from getting their arms all the way around you. That they might try should lead to you wedging your arms open to prevent the bear-hug from closing in the first place.

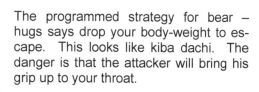

However, if we were that aware of our surroundings then we wouldn't need fighting skills at all. So let's take it that someone got one over on us.

The programmed strategy for bear – hugs says drop your body-weight to escape. This looks like kiba dachi. The danger is that the attacker will bring his grip up to your throat.

We prevent this by grabbing his arm across our body while our other arm injects the elbow into his sternum. The grabbing hand has the added advantage of preventing them from moving away from the blow.

With compliance bought, we can execute the hip throw that we really wanted, bringing the arms to the reverse position and shifting across to aid the throw.

Again, just because we may not be able to get our hands to the end position of the kata shouldn't stop us from having that position as our intention.

A relatively simple variation involves evading that right cross again.

Moving to the outside line, we feed our flinch reaction into a parry that brings the opponent past us.

Our entry keeps us close to the attacker, and the force of his blow is ridden by us and diverted down towards our hip as we maintain contact with *muchimi*.

Our *hikite* hand keeps the attacker's arm pinned against us, and as we breath out we effect an arm-bar.

The swinging elbow comes around at exactly the right time to catch just behind the corner of the attacker's jaw.

The force of our blow and the opponent's disorientation is aided no end by our dropping our bodyweight down by heavily bending our knees. The use of *kibadachi* here goes a long way towards making sure that the circularity of the strike also conforms to what we know of quadrant theory on the attacker. The dropping motion confers new angles on the attacker's body, meaning that we do get to hit "*down on the front*" and "*up on the back*" of the attacker.

Yame.

Heian Yondan

平安四段

HEIAN YONDAN
Peaceful Mind Level Four

This kata has beautiful flowing movements, echoing the qualities of water. One minute it flows quietly and the next it can become a raging torrent.
There are wonderful contrasts between the slow movements and the rapid strikes that follow them.

From a ready position. Sink your weight, look to your left and step out into kokutsudachi. The hands descend sharply to the right with the palms towards the rear.

Slowly raise the arms to a position where the left arm has a vertical forearm, palm forward; and the right arm has a horizontal forearm, palm forward.

This movement has similarities in shape to the opening of Heian Nidan. The feeling is as completely different as the students who learn them at those stages of their development.

Look over your right shoulder and face to the left mirroring the stance and decending palm action. Mirror the rising arms.

Black Belt Tip: The "middle position before the low x-block has crossed wrists. This makes it different to similar positions in Jion and after the jump in Heian Godan. Wind your hip into this movement and the next one so that they work together.

Black Belt Tip: It's easy to slap your elbow, but if your belt doesn't "flick" when you deliver it then no power was generated. Drive your hip, don't just make noise.

Look down the main embusen. Pull up the left foot, crossing the wrists by the right hip. Step out along the embusen into hidari zenkutsudachi making juji gedanbarai.

Step forward into kokutsudachi rotating the crossed wrists around the left hip and make morote uke.

Pull the left foot up whilst both hands come to the right hip. The right fist is palm upward. The left fist is palm rearwards. This is called koshi-gamae.

Kick yoko keage and make uraken. The feeling should be one of placing the foot and fist in the same place.

Without withdrawing it, open the left hand and thrust the right elbow out whilst making zenkutsudachi to the left.

Look over the shoulder, pull the left foot half way to the right, centering your gravity.

Kick yoko keage with the right leg and make uraken.
Open the right hand and thrust the left elbow out whilst making zenkutsudachi to the right. Look to the front.

Sweep the left hand downwards, palm rearwards, and bring the right hand up, palm forwards, in front of the forehead.

Thrust the right hand out to make a palm-upwards shuto uchi (temple height). Bring the left hand up in front of the forehead. At the same time twist the hips quickly to face along the embusen. These last two movements should transfer from one to the other without pause.

Kick maegeri. With the knee still in the air a rolling motion occurs in the arms. Take the right hand down whilst raising the left. Reverse the positions, then

...as the right foot touches down, tuck the left foot in behind to make kosadachi. The right forearm lands uchi komi and the left hand makes hikite. **Kiai.**

Black Belt Tip: There is no jump in this kata. Drive your hips forwards and deliver the power of the descending forearm. Don't just think of the fist as this is not necessarily the focus of the power. The hips sit at a natural angle, not an enforced 45 degrees.

Look over the shoulder. Push the left foot out, and as the hips turn anti-clockwise, make kokutsudachi and kakiwakeuke at a 45° angle to the main embusen.

Kick maegeri, and step in to right zenkutsudachi with oizuki, gyakuzuki. Look to the right.

Black Belt Tip: Kakewake has a feeling of expansion with palms up and then contract with palms down, ready to kick.
Keep hands still while you kick.

Pull the right foot back, and step out at the opposite diagonal to make kokutsudachi and kakiwakeuke.
Kick maegeri, and step out into left zenkutsudachi with oizuki, gyakuzuki.
The wrists are pulled together on the right hip as you look to the main embusen.

Step across onto the embusen with the left foot into kokutsudachi and make moroteuke.

Black Belt Tip: Each morote uke has crossed wrists in between. The feeling should be of winding in and then rolling out.

Step forwards into right kokutsudachi and make moroteuke.

Step forwards into left kokutsudachi and make moroteuke.

Re-position the left foot to make zenkutsudachi and reach forwards with both hands.

Pull the hands down to meet the rising knee. **Kiai.**

The hands become fists just as they pass the knee. Before the foot touches down, look over the shoulder and prepare the arms to face the front again.

Make kokutsudachi and shuto uke.

Step forward into kokutsudachi and shuto uke.

Yame.

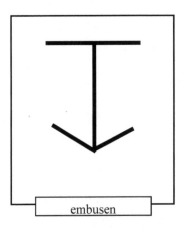

embusen

Applications

The fourth part of this particular learning curve, then, is reserved for those with *some* experience—but not necessarily at a "master" level.

Gedan Awase Teisho-uchi

Let's begin by taking our flinch reaction past an incoming jab or lunge punch.

Without taking up a grip we slap the arm down and momentarily bar the elbow across our body. When this move is performed against someone charging in it can drop them to the floor all by itself—their momentum being their own worst enemy.

Seizing the attacker's wrist, we can pull his arm up high to unbalance him and simultaneously drop our elbow down on his shoulder or chest to increase the idea that he will fall over.

The opening move starts with someone having us in a very vulnerable situation—they have bear-hugged us from behind. Observe how once again the threat level has increased by this stage of learning.

Gedan Awase Teisho uchi, Awase Haiwan uke

We drop our bodyweight to prevent the attacker from lifting us and crushing us with their grip.

By creating a wedge shape in front of us we can momentarily stop an attacker from closing their grasp. Remember that this is not a battle of strength, but a momentary relief to enable the rest of the technique.

By sliding underneath one of the arms and dropping the hands to one of our sides we can effectively use our hip as the base to throw them over; redirecting their intention in a flowing manner around our torso.

If we choose to swiftly pull those hands down then we throw the attacker. Notice how the hip is brought back into play to accomplish this with a fast transition in the kata.

Juji Gedan Barai

With the previous situation we were dealing with a bear hug where we could physically move the attacker—either by guile or speed or knowledge of technique.

This time around, we respond with making the attacker's mechanics work against him.

Should we mange to cross the attacker's arms, then we require a forward motion to drive the attacker completely over the hip and down onto the floor.

There is more going on here than dragging an attacker over your hip. We make their mind switch off by crossing their arms for them. Driving instructors are forever telling students not to cross their hands on the wheel for very good reasons.

Not least of these is that the half of your brain that governs your right hand also governs your right eye; so it is not surprising that when the left eye is given governance of the right hand there is some confusion. We recognise a hand but cannot effectively control it.

Of course, with practice this can be overcome. With concentration the attacker could resist, but who wants to give them time to resist—simply roll them over that hip!

Morote Uke

Following on from the previous move, we look at what happens if they don't fall but instead move around you.

The kata gives us permission to move onwards rather than struggling to achieve a move that has not been possible in this particular confrontation on this particular day. Another time it might have gone sweetly, but now we have to change tactics.

As the attacker has not fallen, we slip our hand between his arm and his body and project it forwards.

Our other hand is used to attach the attacker's arm to us by hitting into it and squeezing it down (this is the "assisting" hand).

Hidden within this move we can feel that our elbows both make contact with the attacker's body.

We cannot emphasise the "leave no gap" principle enough, here, as anyone with any kind of self-preservation instinct is going to wriggle to escape. By locking the attacker's arm against you the attacker will feel more pain as they struggle.

Koshi-gamae

As we saw in Heian Nidan, this "ready positon" can be used to pull someone in towards you. Whereas we previously looked at a reverse punch or "cross", we now use the example of an attacker who has seized our lapel.

Cut through their wrist with your own, rotating their grip outwards and downwards to prevent the attack from continuing. A quick reversal sends the attacker face downwards [principle: give a little to get a little] so that we can lock the elbow as shown before.

Yokokeage, uraken uchi, mawashi empi uchi

Again, just like in Heian Nidan, we raise our knee to impact the attacker's body; we throw our foot out to cave through the attacker's knee; and we strike out towards the attacker's temple or throat with a back-fist strike.

The difference, this time, is that we continue our retaliation with a drive of our hip that sends our elbow colliding with the attacker's temple.

This action is reinforced by our previous hand opening and dragging the attacker's head back into the strike. This makes it a two way action—the attacker's head actually charging into our elbow (with a little assistance).

We know from practice that striking always hurts more if there is a "base" to strike into—in this case it's our hand.

Koshi Gamae

In this case, we have continued the same situation to reflect that final neck-twist which may be necessary in the most extreme situations.

Following the strike with the elbow, the pull on the attacker's neck is accentuated by the way we use our hips when we turn.

The strikes should have bought compliance, so this movement reflects an extreme level of danger to warrant such a lethal response. If the situation doesn't warrant it then there is no need for the retaliations to reach this stage.

Yoko keage, Uraken uchi

This retaliation is the same as before, but with the other side of the body.

Mawashi Empi uchi
As before, this is a simple reversal of the sides of the body.

Gedan shuto uchi

As we find ourselves in close, in a grappling situation, we need to dissuade further aggression escalation very quickly.

As the attacker's hands are busy, our immediate fear is for a head-butt or a knee attack.

Whereas we would rather not get kneed at all, if it had to happen then we must protect the groin. Simply turning the body sideways does a good job in this respect. A knee in the hip hurts, but not nearly as much as a knee in the groin.

This movement also slightly displaces the position of our head– moving it off centre and therefore slightly out of the immediate range of the head-butt. Just to make sure, it is wise that a hand is bought up in front of the forehead to protect you.

At the same time, drop the other hand down to hit into the groin or the inside of the thigh with knife hand strike.

There is a lot to be said for the inside of the thigh as a target for this chop as opposed to the groin. We already know that the human flinch reaction has a pre-determined response away from being struck in the groin; but aside form that we have the femoral nerve and the femoral artery to consider as targets of the thigh which are not protected by anywhere near the same conditioning.

Jodan shuto uchi

Continuing on...

Having bought our attacker's compliance with the previous strike, we bring our hand up to cover the head but on the way we might just give the attacker's head a small nudge backwards to push them away a little and set up our next strike.

As we pivot our hip inwards we can use the "high hand" of the previous combination to strike out into the neck.

It isn't necessarily the edge of the hand that contacts the attacker's neck. The whole arm is thrust forwards with a minimised circular movement that cuts through but also penetrate into the attacker.

The whipping motion is not just with the arms—the hip brings the whole body into play, and as such it delivers the whole bodyweight into the strike.

Maegeri
Continuing on...

We raise our knee, following the wave of our motion forwards.

The knee is brought upwards but also pushed forwards to counter any ideas the attacker's inbuilt flinch reaction would have about protecting his groin.

Immediately we have accomplished our first strike, we continue with a second one as the foot drives out through the attacker's knee.

You don't need to look down to find the attacker's knee, you just need to drive forwards as you do in the kata performance.

As our hands were already in touch with opponent, it is not too difficult to use the hands and feet simultaneously as the hands begin the next short action in this sequence.

Uchikomi

Continuing…

We slide the our right hand to a palm-down position behind the attacker's neck.

The left hand that we had been using to protect our head continues it's outward journey to grind forwards and upwards against the attacker's face.

We then continue that motion to push down. This takes the attacker's head through a tight circle with our right hand as the base or pivot point.

Pulling back (and upwards) with the right hand will either drop them or release your hand ready for the next part of the movement.

Storm forwards striking down with the whole of the forearm. Depending on how much damage the opponent has already suffered will determine what part of your weapon hits the attacker.

You either drop your elbow into their sternum; or trapezius, collarbone or throat—or your forearm folds down into their chest.

Once again we see the descending nature of attacks to the front of the body.

Kakewake uke

Dealing, once again, with that familiar position of the attack already begun; the hands are placed upon you, and this time the attacker has gone straight for a strangle or choke.

If the attacker can reach your neck then there is a good chance that you can reach theirs. If you could not reach their neck then there are numerous strike (e.g.: down on the forearms) that you can do to bring them close enough to use the technique prescribed in Heian Yondan.

In order to strangle them with best effect; we need to cross our arms with our palms upwards and reach up as far as possible into their collar. Taking hold, we use a scissor action to close the blood passageways but leave the attacker's airway clear.
This technique is speeded up with the rotation of the wrists into the neck—having more of an effect than squeezing alone.

This is a fast way to knock them out. Be extra careful in practice.

Notice the movement in the kata shows *how far* we would like to take our hands apart, and use this intention when pulling and wedging our elbows in application.

Maegeri, oizuki, gyakuzuki

We could follow on from the previous section with the same situation, using the strangle to buy time and the percussive techniques to finish the attacker.

We could look at a fresh situation, where anyone grabbing us would immediately get kicked and punched.

We could unite the two ideas, and say that as soon as someone tried to strangle us we would strangle them briefly enough to buy the striking opportunity.

Importantly, raising our knee for percussion should be straight forward—direct. It is followed immediately by the foot projecting straight out. The foot connects with a leg of the attacker's without looking down to find it. The foot connects part of the way through the kicking action, and then proceeds to the full extension position.

The mechanics of the human body mean that the attacker will drop their head forwards while falling backwards.

Our punches could land in any one of a number of anatomically vulnerable areas. Don't overlook the exposed trapezius as this causes a great effect on the opponent.

If the attacker should turn as they fall back then they expose even more targets—like the side of the throat and jaw!

Kakewake uke, maegeri, oizuki, gyakuzuki.
This sequence is repeated and can be used the same way as before.

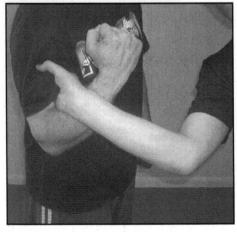

Rotating morote uke

As we try to extricate ourselves from an aggressive situation, the attacker has seized our right bicep with their right hand. This type of grab might come from the side or even the rear, and can be treated the same way.

Curl the right arm around the outside of the attacker's wrist, pulling them in towards us but re-directing their elbow across their body so that the attack cannot continue.

Effectively, we have trapped the attacker's fingers against our arm. Note that our right fist has the thumb turned out (we often see students struggling with the back of their fist turned outwards in this technique—one more rotation has it pegged).

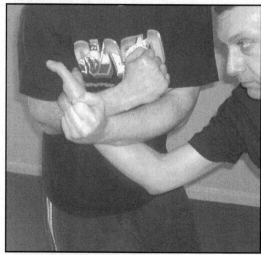

As if this wasn't enough, we help the technique along by curling our left arm across our body and striking down and along the attacker's arm, increasing the pain.

Of course, if the attacker's face should hit our fist or elbow on the way this might be advantageous, too.

We continue the rotation...

If the attacker should fall at this point, then we could move on, or we continue as follows:

Slide the elbow over the attacker's arm and pull them further on. Inject the elbow into the inside of the attacker's bicep/tricep (preferably between them).

As we do all of this we can slide a foot behind the attacker (or maybe even between their legs if we have sufficient leg length). This base might remind us of kokutsudachi.

Rotate both arms across the body to strike and redirect the attacker.

Morote uke

The recurring motif of morote uke presents us with an excellent opportunity to study the move again. We have already seen it in Heian Nidan, Sandan, and now we have multiple occurrences of it in this kata.

There is nothing wrong with only having one useable application for the technique, but we present some more for the sake of finding "the one that works for you".

Shifting to the outside line of an attacker's stepping punch (lunge or jab), we parry and adhere to them to pull them in.

On this occasion we will strike down and across the attacker's body with our elbow. This is helped along by our twisting and pushing the attacker's punching hand back towards them and away (across your body).

This drastically off-balances the attacker.

As they fall away from you, a number of targets become available, so we choose to strike the neck with our thumb knuckle to help them on their way.

Morote uke

A minor variation of the above techniques would see the "grabbing hand" thrust forward with the wrist still ensnared and the other hand striking down on the brachio radialis to effect a similar lock to the one shown in Heian Nidan.

shift stance, reaching.

Once again, as we shift outside of an attack with the fist, we find the attacker's "blind side" or back towards us.

In this situation it is advisable to strike without hesitation, before any further attack becomes possible.

The position from the kata might look like an intermediary stage or a ready position, but is, in fact, quite useful on it's own.

The hands are thrust out, nearly straight forwards, but always with that hint of an arc that brings the hands so close together.

The strike, then, impacts on the carotid sinus of the attacker, using the thumb knuckles and the whole of the inside of the forearms.

There is also, even at this stage of the technique, a small part of the movement that drags the opponent towards you—backwards. Thus, overbalancing them in a manner that they have trouble regaining control over.

Hizageri, shuto uke

Once we achieve a position of strength behind an opponent, our rising knee is directed to the attacker's back.

If we catch the tailbone, this is very painful.

If we catch any higher we run a real risk of permanently damaging the attacker. As such we must be absolutely sure of the necessity of such a move before ever carrying it out.

If we are not able to get completely behind the attacker then a knee to the thigh will do a superb job, anyway.

Our hands assist in this technique by pulling the attacker onto the strike. They keep him off-balance and assist the location and direction of our intended target.

The turn and shuto uke, then marks the absolute escalation of necessity, as we see fit to pass our hands either side of the attacker's head and swiftly return them in the opposite direction.

This is "brain stem twist" at the very least, and more than likely representative of neck-breaking tactics.

Shuto uke

The last shuto uke could be used in the same way as any of the other times this technique has been performed.

The sheer number of times that shuto uke occurs as we travel through kata should tell us something about the essence of our art—the notion of accepting force and still striking forward is an important concept.

If the brain-stem twist shown on the previous page was not enough (?!?) then there is always the principle of continuation logged in this kata as an extra step with the same technique. This reminds us that if the job is not finished then we need to continue until we are once again safe. Twisting the neck sharply one way and then sharply the other is potentially lethal. It occurs at the very end of the kata and lets us know that it is only for the very direst of circumstances (ones which we will hopefully never encounter).

Yame

Return to the beginning, with remaining awareness.

Heian Godan

平安五段

HEIAN GODAN
Peaceful Mind Level Five
The culmination of the Heian family, depicting an amalgamation of the other four, in content and feeling, and showing the first jump that many students learn.
From a ready position
Look to the left, sink your weight and step out into kokutsu dachi making uchi uke.
Immediately make gyakuzuki.
Slowly pull the right foot to the left, look to the right and make kage zuki while looking to your right.

Sink your weight and step to the right into kokutsudachi making uchi uke.
Immediately make gyakuzuki.

Slowly pull the left foot to the right, look forwards and make kage zuki while looking forwards.

Cross the wrists over the left hip and step forwards with the right foot along the main embusen making morote uke in kokutsu dachi.

Step forwards into zenkutsudachi and make juji gedan barai.

Pull the wrists back sharply.

Thrust the open hands upwards, with the wrists crossed, juji age uke.

Black Belt Tip: Your elbows must be spread wide enough to allow you to see. Straight arms would go higher, but would prevent you from seeing the attacker.

Uncross the wrists and pull down to the right hip. The right hand is palm up, fingertips forward; the left hand is palm down, fingertips pointing to the right.

Push the left hand sharply forwards then step into zenkutsudachi and punch oi zuki chudan. **Kiai**

Turn 180° anti-clockwise, pivoting on the left foot. Make kiba dachi and gedan barai. [Some teachers have a fumi komi just prior to the gedan barai]

Black Belt Tip: For a smooth performance, take your hand *over* your head from the previous position. Swinging the hand around the front of your body takes longer and does not promote the effective winding up of the hips necessary to drive the technique.

Cross the arms in front of the body, left hand under. Look to the left, pull the right fist back to the hip as the left hand pushes slowly around. The left palm is horizontal until the last moment when it turns over.

Make mikazuki geri with the right foot to the left hand and then set down into kiba dachi while making empi.

Black Belt Tip: Do not allow your hikite hand to drift away form your hip during the fumikomi. This makes your elbow strike short and sharp, and you are more likely to use your hip to deliver it.

Look to the right. Move the left foot to make kosa dachi and make morote uchi komi.

Make jodan morote urazuki, twisting the hips and head to face the other way. The left foot is placed naturally, not forced into any stance.

Jump from the left foot, upwards and 180° anti-clockwise. While in the air, **Kiai.**

Black Belt Tip: Although it feels good, don't take a run up for the jump. Think "*knees up to the chest*" or risk just tucking your heels up behind you.

Land in kosadachi, making juji gedan barai.

Look to the right and step out with the right foot to make morote uke in zenkutsudachi.

Look over the left shoulder. Move the left foot across, sweeping the left hand down and the right hand to just in front of the forehead.

Change the stance to a forward facing zenkutsudachi and thrust the right hand downwards (palm uppermost) while bringing the left hand to right ear.

Move the left foot across to the right in order to make kokutsudachi and manji gamae.

Slowly move the left foot directly backwards to the right foot.

Black Belt Tip: Notice the weight changes and shifts of your belt as you perform. Keep the movements alive rather than allowing them to drift off as the kata comes towards it's end.

Twist the body and feet on the spot, repeating the same move on the other side of the body.

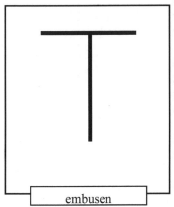

embusen

Cut downwards with the right hand, the left hand just in front of the forehead.

Step forwards with the right leg into zenkutsudachi, thrusting the left palm downwards (palm uppermost) and the right palm to the left ear.

Move the right foot to make kokutsudachi and make manji gamae.

Step backwards to Yamae.

Applications

Uchiuke

An attacker jabbing towards our face might represent any kind of incoming hand. Our channelled flinch response is used to access the blind side of the opponent whilst simultaneously keeping us safe.

The idea of sticking to the opponent's limb is used to control their balance and pull them in while momentarily preventing any kind of further attack. There is huge leverage available with the attacker's elbow locked against our chest—we use it to angle the attacker's body and weapons away from us.

The outbound fist is used to impact with the thumb knuckle into the attacker's shoulder where the deltoid meets the pectoralis minoris. Our hikite and their elbow at the middle of our chest are used to provide the base for the lock.

Should the attacker's head hit your fist, too, then we get a bonus shot.

Gyakuzuki

The close range of the reverse-punch takes it past the attacker's limb directly to the weak points in the ribs, or, if you can reach, to the sternum itself.
The use of an unbalancing pull with the other hand often leaves the sternum open to attack.

Kage zuki

The movement is continued by manoeuvring behind the attacker to pull them to you.
The forearm is angled slightly down in order to control the attacker's balance and the hikite hand restrains one of their arms. It is quite possible to choose whether to stress the opponent's windpipe (strangle) with your radius or their blood passageways.

We can close the attacker's windpipe by pulling directly towards our own chest (effectively trying to crush it). We could choose to choke by rubbing more across the throat giving us greater control of the blood vessels rather than the airway.

In practice, be careful not to rise onto your toes. If the attacker is taller than you then they must come down to your height rather than you losing your balance. Pull them in.

Alternative Kage zuki:

If a choke seems like too forceful a response, you could always choose to merely control their balance via the attacker's elbow.

Once we are able to avoid an incoming arm (whether it be push, attempted grab, or any kind of punch) and we actively seek out the outside line, we use the muchimi method illustrated in the koshi-gamae techniques of Heian Nidan and Heian Yondan to draw the attacker's wrist back to our hip.

With the attacker's palm aimed upwards their elbow will be accessible and we use their own balance against them to keep them down.

The downward pressure and revolved wrist make variable pressure to the elbow a very effective control technique.

A minor variation would see the opponent pulled in towards us and set in a hammer lock (as in Heian Sandan). This shows us how the family of kata are culminating in a last lesson that reminds us fully of the prior four parts.

Uchi uke, Gyakuzuki, Kage zuki

The techniques can also be used on the other side of the body.

Morote uke
This technique can be used exactly the same way as previously demonstrated.

Juji Gedan Barai

As we try to leave a confrontation, the attacker seeks to pull us back in. Without waiting for the rest of their attack, we need to take care of the attached wrist and cause a momentary shut down of their intention.

Plunging the thumb knuckle through the wrist of the attacker causes their grip to either release entirely, or at least to disrupt any pulling motion that they had planned.

Take note of the location of the strike. The creases in the skin look like a small chain runs around your wrist. We need to strike close to the edge, pinching nerves against the ulna bone and towards the edge of the wrist.

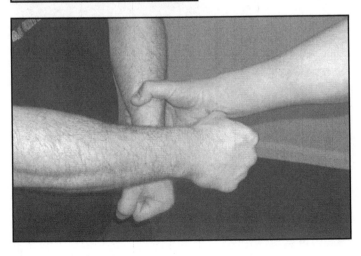

Pull up

The movement continues by hooking the fist under the attacker's wrist and drawing it towards you with the palm up.

There is nothing wrong with pulling it in with the palm down—it's just not what we're showing here.

The leverage on the attacker's elbow is used to gain control over them.

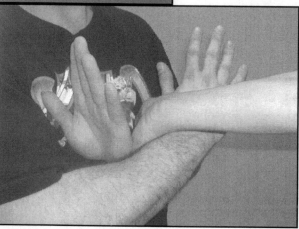

In practice, never go beyond the point where your training partner rises onto their toes. Anything more than this has the whole of their bodyweight hanging from the shoulder joint. This particular joint is held in place more by suction than, say, the ball and socket of the hip joint, and as such is more prone to injury.

Juji Age Uke

The kata has us throw the hands completely up in the air, sure to wreck the attacker's shoulder.

Note that the control of the attacker rests in the little finger side of their hand. This is the part that you must retain and concentrate on pressing at the desired angle and direction.

In practice allow your partner to ease down before you raise your hands, for their own protection.

 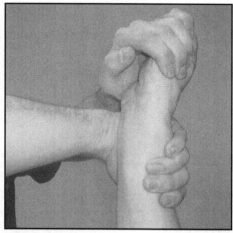

 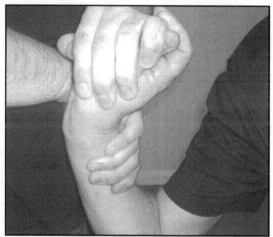

In this complicated little sequence, the attacker's arm is controlled and pulled around so that they fall to their knees.

In our example, the right hand traps the attacker's wrist, but the left hand has the real control. It is by pushing on the "little-finger" side of the attacker's hand that we get the maximum leverage and give direction to our technique.

The hands do not quite get to the position that is familiar from the kata—the attacker's wrist is in the way. That doesn't mean that we shouldn't try to get there. In fact it is the intention of taking the move further than keeps us in control when the adrenaline has hit us and our fine motor skills are reduced.

To complete the sequence, if it was necessary, we could take hold of the attacker's head and produce the target that we require.

The punch will either impact to the face or the throat.

With a full forward step we drive our whole bodyweight into the punch.

Don't overlook the importance of the step, either. The "C" shape that is drawn on the floor helps to protect the groin as we step into the attacker. Offensively, the step is used to kick and trample the attacker on our way forward.

Taking another look at the previous sequence, we can find further uses for the individual parts of the whole.

Juji gedan barai

Taking an attacker's hook punch with our soft-block, we cover the attack and enter into their area.

Our forward drive takes our elbow high into the attacker's chest (or maybe their throat). This could be enough on it's own, but we must be ready to carry on if it is necessary.

Our hand snakes around the attacker's arm, pinning it to his side, and makes a thumb knuckle strike to the kidney in an upward direction.

At the same time our forward momentum is used to drive our right arm down and over the attacker's shoulder giving them direction to fall towards the floor.

Potentially, we can break the opponent's collarbone, here, tear the rotator cuff, and if we ere lucky enough to catch the jaw at the same time we could do even more damage.

Juji Age uke

Throw the body to the outside of an attack, even if it means ducking a roundhouse punch.

Slice the right hand up underneath the attacker's arm to the opposite side of their neck.

This keeps your shoulder tightly under their arm and causes it to rise against one side of their neck while you attack the other.

With the initial strike in place, buying us precious seconds, we throw the other arm up behind the attacker's back until we can feel our own wrist. This means that we can achieve our result without having to <u>see</u> it.

Both wrists are pulled towards our heart—making sure to keep below the level of the attacker's centre of gravity.

The attacker is choked by their own shoulder on one side (providing a base) and our forearm rolling down and into the attacker's neck on the other side.

Push, oizuki

Following on from the prior situation, we can pull the head down to our side. This has the advantage of affecting the attacker's balance—their subconscious desire not to be thrown to the floor leaves them without the inclination to attack. This is on top of any effect we might have on their neck.

Our action is multiplied, then, by subsequently trapping the attacker's arm and pulling it around our body (therefore whipping their head back the other way).

As we do this we can direct our fist forwards. What looks like a punch can often end up striking the attacker with the forearm or even bicep. If the fist does hit anything on it's course, it will be a downward motion in relation to the angle of the body, and our most likely areas to land on are down the central line and therefore over the most vulnerable organs.

Once again, the stepping motion is used to propel our weight into the thrust of the arm. This is vital or we are left with mere arm strength.

We are much stronger punching with the weight of our body thrust forward by our leg strength.

Fumikomi, gedan barai

In any grappling situation there will be movement and struggle. There is a tendency to let the situation overtake you and play by the attacker's rules. We must have learned by this stage that we must, in any confrontation, change the situation to one that favours us.

By striking/slapping into the attacker's face or ear we gain our momentary advantage. Then it is necessary to move fast so that control of the situation is not regained by the attacker.

Wrap your arm around the attacker's neck, securing their face (looking away from you) with your bicep and forearm. Making the attacker look away means that they have a much harder time hitting you and they are easier to manipulate ar they cannot predict your actions.

Knee into the inside of the thigh, in the area of the highly vulnerable femoral artery.

.

Continue the motion through the leg and spin yourself so that you momentarily make a reverse guillotine.

Tear your hand in a downward motion that resembles gedan barai.

If you maintain hold of the attacker's face/jaw with the hikite hand then you will have made extra damage.

Note that the use of stance is once again all about dropping the opponent downwards, and that in doing so we are encouraged to keep our back up straight to prevent the situation from deteriorating into a grapple on the floor.

Hirate uke

We have, by now, assimilated that attacks with the arms are similar in how they can be handled.

Whether the attacker has pushed or punched; whether it was straight or hooking, we can find our way to this position.

We have attached the attacker's wrist and pulled it across our body. At the same time we take our other arm outwards.

If there is an impact on the neck then this is extra.

The arm goes out across the throat. The attacker can resist falling right up until the point where we rotate the palm to forward facing. This subtle turn, while gauging into the attacker's windpipe, is enough to finally break their balance.

The stance is used for our own stability, and to encourage downward motion. The part that most people miss is the importance of the hikite hand. Pulling the attacker's arm across the body can produce an effective arm-bar all on it's own. This is especially true if the practitioner has good control of the tension of their chest and stomach area. A little outward breath here can add to the pain the attacker feels.

Mikazuki geri

When the grapple has begun, it can be wise to try to make some space between your body and that of the attacker. For the most part this can be accomplished by pushing and pulling, but also with how you arrange your feet and your behind. Dropping down and out might appear unbalanced, but it goes a good way towards preventing a bear-hug and a good many close-in strikes.

We use the same posture to allow us to attack the opponent's knee from the inside in a crescent motion.

Note the location of the opposite hand in helping the attacker to lose their balance when the knee is taken out from below them. If we manage to maintain hikite then it is even easier.

Mawashi empi

Sliding the hand behind the attacker's head, we secure it and pull it on to our swinging elbow.

More important that where the strike lands (although usually this will be the temple or the cheekbone) is the idea that it lands with the force of the body inwards and downwards towards the "capping hand".

Morote uke/morote uchikomi

The situation moves on with another "what if?" scenario.

We take it that more retaliation is necessary in order to prevent further attack. In some way our actions so far have not had the desired effect.

Sliding the hand of the striking arm over the attacker's face we can keep him pressed downwards. Our fingers open and hook under his jaw.

While our other hand and arm maintain or pull on the attacker's shoulder or neck, we rotate the inner hand in a small circle outwards.

This neck crank is obviously severe and in practice the partner must be allowed to roll out of the movement.

In the kata the arm movements are accompanied by a shift over to the side. This dynamically adds your bodyweight to the movement.

If you should happen to catch the opponent's leg with your hooking leg then they will have their full bodyweight placed into the neck-lock.

Jodan morote urazuki

If we treat the previous morote uke as a strike, as shown elsewhere in this book, then we still might be encouraged to think of kosa dachi as capturing the attacker's leg.

The apparent assisted punch is categorised by a couple of strange bits of code that can help our understanding of kata greatly.

Looking away from the attacker suggests that the effect we are looking for occurs away from them.

Twisting the hip contra to the direction of the "punch" leads us to look at the effect more closely as the emphasis is not of strength "into the opponent"..

The hip is produced as a base for the attacker to fall over. The upward motion with the arm is resisted by the "assisting arm" and the attacker is thrown.

Of course, any pain that they have from the hand at their throat increases the attacker's compliance considerably.

Note: we have practiced this throw with the use of crashmats and high jump mats, and can attest that even with lots of protective equipment there is still pain.

This is a good reason for having something "indicated" in performance rather than continually

Principle
Representative. The jump itself represents something that happens to someone else. The move is hidden.

Jump

If you perform the movement with enough force (say, so much that you tried to leave the floor yourself) then the attacker is thrown. As a memory aid for leaving the floor, the *performance* is one where we leave the floor!

Upon landing the opponent, we have many options.

Please note that the crouching position maintains a vertical spine. Bending over might lead to us being dragged to the floor or overbalancing. On mats a good grapple is fun, but "in the street" there are plenty of reasons not to. We don't want to be rolling around with needles and other substances on the floor if we can prevent it.

The knees are also used to help maintain control of the attacker.

Juji gedan barai

The simplest application is to keep the attacker's arm pinned against you while you strike them.

For control and compliance, we might choose to hook that arm back down towards the attacker. Bracing their elbow against our chest we apply a

Morote uke

The good old "assisted block" appears again. The frequency of it's use should alert us to the importance and versatility of the posture. Yet you will not see people using it in free-sparring. This is simply because the applications of it are not suitable for competition.

Adapting to the situation and making our way to the blind side of the attacker, we begin to choke him in a similar way to the "kage zuki" application at the beginning of the kata.

The attacker manages to take his arm forward, so before we lose the situation entirely, we must redirect him.

Folding his hand up to his own shoulder, we secure it with the arm across his throat.

Our other hand is taken to his elbow, which we proceed to compress towards the attacker's own wrist and our chest.

In this way we have joint manipulation and simultaneous choke which is enhanced by the attacker's own limb.

The stance is used to drive the hips forward below the lock/choke to unbalance the opponent.

Now, a lot of people would not choose to bend forward to find a low target, and we would agree with them. What if you were already low down? What if you had just escaped from a headlock?

Gedan shuto uchi

If we mange to avoid the attacker's lunge and grab or punch and move to the outside line, we might still choose to strike to the inside line.

The high hand pulls on the attacker's arm, extending it, breaking his balance and causing some resistance and tension with the rest of his body. He is "primed" for striking.

While bracing the attacker by placing a foot behind their lead leg, we chop downwards. This strike might not hit the groin due to the male reflexive action, but it might *because* of the previous distractions.

The redundancy built into the strike is the circular nature of the movement, leading the hand ot the inside of the thigh should it fail to make the groin.

Gedan hira shuto uchi

The continuation of the movement takes the left hand upwards to unbalance and strike the attacker while the right hand cuts down to repeat the first strike.

The important part here is the reversal of the bodyweight, from pulling to driving forward.

Manji Gamae

A simple unbalancing act continues the previous technique as we pull on the attacker's leg while striking them in a descending manner with the other hand.

Small additions can make a big difference. With the hand on the inside thigh, try taking hold of flesh and twisting—it's a sure way to buy compliance and avoid having to use strength to lift the assailant.

The front foot moves across and your weight is shifted from front to back. This makes the front foot dislodge the attacker's balance even further; even if you are unable to actually "sweep" the attacker's leg.

Hira shuto uchi

Accepting the attacker's massive right hook, we cut it off in it's prime by entering into the force of it. Our soft block covers the arm and our flinch reaction means that we have the other hand up covering our head.

Immediately strike the back of the attacker's head with a ridge hand strike. If you are brave enough then you can lock your head against the opponent's to provide extra shock to the strike.

This could be enough to knock the attacker out, but in order to follow through, we take our raised, flinching, hand and thrust it forwards and down.

Wherever this strike hits will be good. The path down the centre-line includes great targets like the bridge of the nose, the chin, the throat, the sternum, etc.

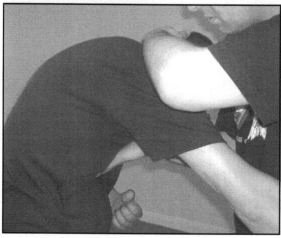

The spiralling motion of the downward strike, contrasted with the rising strike and the forceful positioning of the body make this a particularly useful technique.

The following could follow on directly from the previous pages, or, obviously, it could be used as a stand-alone technique from any in-close situation.

Manji gamae, and stand up slowly.

One of the simplest uses for manji gamae is the neck rip.

Simply place one hand behind the attacker's head and the other by the opposite side of their jaw. The hands are diametrically opposed to each other.

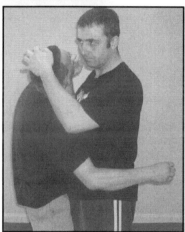

The hand are moved in equal and opposite rotations past each other, but with the attacker's head being manipulated by the movement.

Fast movement is damaging, but slow movement can exist to control and restrain the attacker.

Note that once again the work of the application is done long before the "final" position.

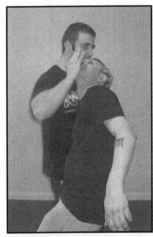

Turning Manji gamae

Again, we could follow on immediately by looking at that principle that was one of our initial findings in the first kata. Add an angle.

If we have not succeeded with our technique in adjusting the attacker's neck with our simple rotation methods, then we add an angle by twisting our own body as we rotate the hands back the other way.

Remember, if one rotation won't do it you can always try again, but if you have to try again you need to also do something different or you will only have the same result.

It should not need saying, at this point in a student's development, that practice with a partner must be very careful. The spine is a wonderful thing, but far too easy to injure, and recovery from spinal injury is never as complete as one would like.

Shuto uchi combinations, manji gamae

These can be used exactly as before from the other side of the body.

Yame

Conclusions

If kata is to be anything more than a form of dance then it must have applications. If Karate is to survive as anything other than a stylised sport it is our duty to reflect upon the movements and the meanings, and to make our practice the practice of the application. There are more applications than we have presented here. Some of them are more efficient, some of them are more destructive; the one that have been shown have been the ones that fitted with the idea of this book.

In most schools, the study of the Heian kata is relegated to "something that must be undertaken in order to pass the next examination".

With only three months or so between grades it becomes increasingly difficult to provide adequate time and tuition for the applications and deeper aspects of the study of Kata and Karate.

As "serious" Karate-ka, then, we must make it our duty to look deeper and practice those old principle-led applications thoroughly. The Heian Kata can be our guide, bringing us back to a base to re-examine from whenever we might lose our way.

How can we trust the Heian Kata to be our guide, when it is a modern set of Kata? Let's take it on trust that Master Itosu used a set of the finest movements as the basis for the creation of these kata. "Advanced" Karate-ka who know the Kanku Dai, Bassai Dai, Jion, Meikyo kata etc. can vouch that the movements of the Heian Kata are taken from those supposedly older kata.

The practice of the exercise as callisthenics for school children in no way invalidates the usefulness of the movements (but perhaps it does invalidate the method of practice if all you are interested in is self defence).

Take the modern phenomenon of "Aerobic Kick-boxing" and "Aerobic Karate". These exercise-based activities do not diminish Boxers or kickboxers. The movements are still valid as they were originally intended to be. The difference is the delivery method of the tuition and the intention of the modern practitioners. They want the exercise but they don't want to fight. The difficulty only arises when one of the aerobic students thinks they can fight just by the nature of the name of the activity they practice. Maybe they can fight—either through natural instinct or by further researching the origins of their art to find it's fighting back-ground—but they didn't get that ability from their aerobic practice.
So it is with us and Kata.

A well respected instructor once told this author that "practicing kata just makes you good at doing kata". My argument is that it depend what you mean by "practising kata". Don't just learn the steps, the force and tempo of movements; take the time to find out the applications. Find applications as they apply to your reality (not just fantasy retaliations against fantasy attacks).

This method of learning (retro-engineering) may be completely the opposite of the original practices. It is thought that original practitioners in Okinawa would have been taught the techniques, taught the targets, and then summarised their learning into the mnemonic known as Kata.

Most of us do not have the luxury of learning that way. We have syllabi that produce regular examinations and new belt colours without regard for the depth of learning of the practitioner.

As Black Belts we may find that we have time on our hands as the time lapse between grades gets longer or ceases. At this stage we must validate our knowledge and our grade by revisiting all the information that we have and making sure that it fits with what we know of real assaults and our ability to respond to those assaults.

Those old Karate Masters who espoused such wisdom as "learning never ceases" were right, weren't they?

So what is it that the Heian series teaches us?

Well, we seem to have uses for it depending upon our needs. As students of self defence we investigate self defence moves found within the kata. We have found locks, throws, strikes, kicks, and chokes and strangles. We have found release from situations as diverse as hook punches, straight punches, grabs, grapples, strangles, and bear-hugs. In this way we have found our peace of mind.

The regular practice in increasing increments of aggression and response have led us (or can lead us) to feel that we have the ability to cope with these situations. The desensitisation to violent conflict has led us to be wary and aware without being scared of these situations. Our ability to harm the human body has led us to a degree of control and wariness about our own abilities. As proficiency increases it becomes a part of regular practice to find ways of *not* hurting training partners rather than wishing we were *able* to hurt them.

We have found moving meditation.

We have found an introspective art that provides camaraderie and causes us to question our motivation in training and our place in the world. The answers to our questions continue to direct us towards that old maxim "there is no place to hide in a gi".

We find an honesty with ourselves that reflects how deep we search. We recognise and come to terms with our limitations.

We are humbled by any praise no matter how well earned for we realise that there is still far to go.

Kata practice, indeed. For some it will be superficial, for some it will be a Peaceful Mind.

Keep searching.

Appendices

Karate instructors often count with the words ichi, ni, san, chi, and goh for 1-5 in Japanese, but the kata are not named the same way.

Interestingly, *Shodan* means First level, but *Nidan* means Level Two. *Sandan* is Level Three, *Godan* is Level Five, but *Yondan* is Fourth Level.
This has to do with good manners in not naming something (a kata in this case) with something that sounds like the Japanese word for "death". So *Chidan* become *Yondan*, and *Shichidan* (Level Seven) becomes *Nanadan* (Seventh Level). Shodan rather than Ichidan is because we have first instead of one—like beginning (shoshin—beginners' mind).

I was told this by a Japanese instructor. A visitor to my dojo from Osaka said that she had never heard such nonsense.

Terminology

Age uke rising receiver
Bunkai analysis
Chudan middlelevel
Dan degree grades
Embusen performance line
Funakoshi Gichin the name of the founder of Shotokan
Gedan barai low level sweep
Godan level 5
Hanmi half-on
Heian Peace
Hidari left
Hikite returning hand
Itosu Ankoh the teacher of master Funakoshi
Kake hooking
Karate do The way of the Empty Hand
Kata form
Kiai everything together
Kihon basics

Kokutsudachi back stance
Kyu low grades.
Migi right
Muchimi sticking
Naore/enoi relax
Nidan level 2
Oizuki lunge thrust
Oyo application
Sandan level 3
Satori enlightenment
Shodan level one
Shomen the front
Shoshin beginners' mind
shotokan The Hall of "Pine Waves"
Shuto uke sword hand receiver
Tettsui uchi hammerfist strike
Yamae return to ready position
Yoi ready
Yondan fourth level
Zenkutsudachi front stance

Kihon

Often referred to as *"Basics"*, this kata remains an exquisite view of Karate. The apparent simplicity of the movements begs for further study. The word itself actually means fundamental, and the old name of the kata, **Taikyoko sono ichi**, or **Taikyoko Shodan** can be taken as *Great Universal, first cause*, or *level one*.

The youngest of the kata, Master Funakoshi is said to have created this one for students who were having difficulty with the Heians. Let's remember that the students he was teaching in the 1920s were University students. They probably didn't have much of a problem learning Heian Shodan, particularly after the order had been rearranged.

I suspect that the answer is much more in-depth. Funakoshi was aware of the reliance on **Sanchin** kata by the Goju ryu and related Naha-te schools as a principle method of teaching. In the Shorin ryu the kata accorded the same level of importance had traditionally been the **Naihanchi** or **Tekki** kata. Now, this one *might* have been too difficult for a beginner, impatient to train, to sweat, and to begin using their techniques. In his wisdom, Master Funakoshi created Kihon kata. It was probably created in order to drill students. In naming this kata, the master tells us what he intended.

It is simple because everything should be simple. The more complicated you make your techniques the more likely they are to fail you. It includes turns in all directions, continually covers the vital centre-line of the body. The techniques that it contains, **gedan barai** and **oizuki** can be used in multiple ways.

If you learn a new principle, say hip vibration, and you cannot apply it with Kihon kata then there is no way that you will apply it with Bassai Dai. As such, Black Belt students are continually brought back to study Kihon—completing the circle of learning and beginning again.

Dr Clive Layton first coined the term, I believe, *The Taikyoko Principle*. It's one that I like to use and one which has a great deal of significance for all true Karate-ka.

Kihon

Kihon

PRINCIPLES

Remember:

- **If you can avoid the confrontation, do.**
- **If you can talk your way out of it before it gets messy, do.**
- **If you can hit then escape, pre-emptively or otherwise, do.**
- **If you hit an attacker and it doesn't finish it then use the time you buy yourself to use your technique. An aggressor will be more compliant if you have already hit him.**
- **If one technique does not fulfil your requirements use another. Don't stop. Carry on until you are safe. Kata applications show a snap shot of action, not the whole fight.**
- **If you can, move to a position of relative safety/strength (off-line rather than directly in front of his "other" fist).**
- **Safety first. Practice the moves with speed, power, and visualisation only on a bag or thin air, not on a partner. This is what kata are for. When practicing on empty air don't lock out joints, use your muscles to stop the movement.**

Awareness. Be aware of your situation. Your surroundings, potential threats. *During* a confrontation– as soon as contact is made you can find any other part of the assailant.

Distance. The attacker begins at a realistic distance to attack you, or they aren't actually attacking you.

Common Attacks. If the attack isn't the kind that people normally do then there is little reason to prepare for it. There are enough real types of attack for us to learn to deal with without creating fantasy ones.

Pre-Emption If possible, and morally/legally correct, always advisable. Action beats reaction. **Pre-emption**. When you feel that there is no other alternative, then using what you know before the other person gets the chance to attack you might be all that you have.
It isn't necessarily a strike, though hitting pre-emptively might be sound advice.
The strike might be considered a stun, buying you time to do the technique that you favour; in which case we label it **BAR**—body alarm reaction.

Off-line It is best to have your centre-line aimed at the opponent and to have theirs aimed away from you! This makes it harder for them to aim any of their "weapons" at you.

Shock (BAR) Dealing with the "adrenaline dump", and causing the shock to occur others. All tactics take place after BAR (Body

Alarm Reaction) has been caused.

Mind, Breath, Body. In that order. Intention, energy, then the physical movement.

KI

Focus on the "One Point" All power comes from the
dantien/tanden/belly.

All force directed to the centre. Aim everything you
have towards the centre of the opponent for depth of penetration.

All limbs in motion/active Always strike with more than one limb. Your feet
are a part of the technique, even if they don't appear to be.

Quadrant Theory Yin-yang taken three-dimensionally.

Unite mind breath and body. Only with full intention, breathing and physical
body will a technique come together to best effect.

Pressure Points The last 5% of any given technique.

Redundancy. Should your chosen technique only *half* succeed then you need to
know that it will be *enough*. The best techniques are those that, should they miss
their mark, still do what you intended. **Redundancy.** Even when the technique
might not live up to your full expectations, it will serve a purpose.

Five-Phase Theory To get the best out of T.O.M., you should follow
the Law of 5 Elements.

Adapt. Should one technique not succeed to the fullest extent then quickly move
on to another. The idea of flow is paramount. **Adaptability.** Whatever techniques make up your arsenal must be useful for more than one situation.

Stances are the application of bodyweight to finish a tech-
nique. The stance is the last part of any technique, not the first. **Bodyweight.** To
use our bodyweight against someone is to add to our strength.
Thrusting bodyweight forwards is the use of a front stance.

Balance. Everything you do must affect an attacker's balance while maintaining your own.
If the attacker is unbalanced they will not possess their full capability.

Locking Lore

Leave No Gap Any space between your limb and the opponent
will present a weakness.

Controlled Pliability   Tension prevents movement, so we remain able to move, but without becoming flaccid. We need to control where and when we are pliable.

Give a little to get a little.   In order to pull someone who is very strong or resisting, it may be necessary to let them momentarily pull in their direction so that we can then pull in ours.

Hand to your heart.   Pulling your hand towards your heart is your strongest mechanical movement. Your whole body, every muscle, is made to *pull*. You don't have a pushing muscle.
Pulling towards you has the added advantage of hyper-extending the grasp of anyone who has seized you.

Multiple Angles.   Taking a technique (any technique) through multiple angles and planes makes it more effective.

Both Hands Work.   In every single technique, both hands have a function. No hand comes back to your body without something attached. If it's not *pulling*, leave it out in front.

Complex torque   The human body can resist one directional force, but 3?

Base.   All joint locks need a base or they will fail.

Variable Pain.   When any lock is placed, vary the intensity to keep it viable. Constant pain can be resisted.

Small Circle Big Result   Centrifugal force, and the ability to use the smallest lever to move the biggest object.

Cross-body motor reaction. Pulling on one side of the body has an equal and opposite reaction upon the other side of the body. We can use this to our advantage by causing the Pre-Determined Response that negates any instant further attack.

Give a Little to Get a Little   Direct force often needs to be slightly absorbed before it can be resisted.

Monkey Grip. The fingers wrap around, and if the thumb "happens" to engage then that's fine, but we don't deliberately attempt to engage the thumb.

This grip should not involve conscious thought or fine motor skills. As such, we should be able to use it even under stressful conditions.

Hitting Cannon

Heavy Hand　　　　　　　　Always penetrate, never bounce off.
Heavy Hand.　　　　　　　All strike are designed to penetrate. Striking *through* a target is better than striking the surface.

Soft & Hard, Targets & Weapons. Where the weapon you are using is bony, it should be used against soft targets. Where the weapon you are using is soft, it should be used against hard targets.

Placing hard weapons against hard targets usually leads to one of them getting broken—and it might be your weapon!

Soft weapons against soft targets leads to absorption of force in two directions, negating some of the effect.

Waveform　　　　　　　　The motion of any strike is a figure of 8/ infinity loop.

Front=Down, Back=Up.　　When we make contact with an opponent, if the contact is to the front of the body there should be a downward angle on it. Contact to the back of the body should have an upward angle to it for maximum disruption.

The Kata Code

Space Between.　　　　　Although in performance the arms touch, that doesn't mean you can't place something (like a head) between them.

An Open Hand is an Elbow.　Whereas the closed fist drawn to your side signifies a wrist that has been grabbed, the open hand identifies that you have an opponent's elbow. The evidence is that if you place an opponent's wrist at your hip their elbow will usually end up in front of your solar plexus. The different hand position shows how much harder it is to close your grasp around an elbow and also the idea of trapping the forearm with your own. The open hand does not rely upon a grip with the fingers to be effective.

Kick Height.　　　　　　Although the kick in performance might be jodan, the target will be gedan. Our aim is to strike with enough power to "achieve" jodan!

Height Change.　　　　　Standing up and moving forward takes our

weight in a whole new direction.
See how dropping or pushing or pulling would not have the same effect.

Obvious Weapon?   Not Necessarily the most Obvious
Weapon.

Flow   See how the changes in stance
are used to change from pulling to pushing to dropping the opponent.
See how they **Link.**

Slow Moves.   They represent something to do
with the lethality of the technique or the difficulty of applying it, and usually both.

Representative.   The jump itself represents something that happens to someone else. The move is hidden.

Methods

Impact, seizing, controlling

Blood, Nerves, Airways, Concussive force, Joint manipulation (levers, hinges), tearing

Location, Tool, Angle, Direction, Intensity,

The moves of the kata reflect retaliations conducted on an attacker. The movements do not exist to block an attack, but rather to leave the defender in a better position (preferably with the attacker unable to continue).

Application Principles

We don't just want you to learn what we have to say; we seek to empower learners to discover applications for themselves. In this way we return to Funakoshi sensei's maxim that one doesn't need to know many kata; just to know a few really well. It is perfectly possible to take the principles and apply them to any kata, regardless of style, for workable applications.
We don't know the original applications—no-one alive today does. The arts have not been handed down complete but as methods of movement. Anyone who claims to have the original applications is actually showing *their* interpretation and understanding of their kata.
All kata applications today are "*reverse engineered*" - i.e.: the movement has been analysed (**bunkai**) until its method of use (**oyo**) has been revealed. Those who are teaching applications that were passed down to

them have only repeated someone else's bunkai-oyo jutsu.

Just because the kata consists of fists does not limit the application.
The kata movement is what happens *after* the initial engagement.
There are *no blocks* in kata. All kicks make contact *below* the belt.
All chudan punches are to the *head*. We do not begin in a stance or "on guard", merely aware.
The responses are to attacks that commonly occur, at a distance where there is a real danger (unlike so many sparring practices where the distance is only applicable to a touch).
The kata does not reflect directions to face waiting opponents in, but directions to displace opponents to.
The end point is the dead point, the action occurs in the middle.
The weapon is not always the end of the limb.
Kata applications have surface (*omote*) and hidden (*ura*) applications.

You should feel free to add your own "laws" to the above, based on what you find when you train. Using keys like these provides a shorthand way of referring to an idea, and when those you train with share the same language then it cuts down on explanation time and allows everyone to grasp similar principles based on existing knowledge (e.g. "I want you to apply this lock with a *heavy hand*, just as if you had punched").

Whilst the above principles have all proven true in our research, there is one principle that holds sway over all the others—
There is always an exception to the rule!

The basic shape made by the first kata reflects the letter "I" that students are familiar with, having an additional pair of "wings" on the top. In the second kata there are additional "wings" at the bottom. The third kata is reduced to a "T" shape, and the fourth a descending arrow. The fifth kata then is simply a "T" shape again.

If the shapes are transposed onto one another then they look remarkably like the kanji for "Heian". What relevance has this? Well, it might be one reason for the turns being in the directions that they are. If the kata is considered as a moving meditation then it could become a part of the practice that the karate-ka draws out a "Peaceful mind" with their body.

平
安

Some things you might like to consider are the number and type of turns in each kata. Notice how often we add up 360 degrees or multiples of it. Notice how each turn in the kata will take you through North, East, South and West and how these things link together.

If the kata were symbolic of Bhuddist monks' practice methods then consider that the turns may have been to offer prayer in each direction, to be protected in each direction, to cast out imperfections in each direction, and to allow the state of mind of a practitioner to pass from their worldly thoughts due to complex stepping rituals. Consider that as a code of exercise the kata make these turns habitual. They are telling you to face all directions, to turn in any direction.

Every move takes you through multiple angles. There are no "linear movements".

As noted earlier, the number five is significant to the Oriental superstition. In no way should the word superstition be construed negatively, it is just a description of a way of thought beyond the common Occidental mindset.

The **Five Realms** (usually translated as Five Rings) from the book by *Miyamato Musashi* dictates a philosophy and a path through life coloured by the Elements of Zen thought. They are Wood, Fire, Earth, Water, and the Void.

The five realms are named after so called "elements", and oriental medicine also thinks of the body as affected by different "phases" of energy (ki) which share most of the elemental names as the "realms". The difference is **Void**,

 fire

 water

 earth

wood

metal

which is not represented as a type of *ki* in the body, but **Metal** is. One has to wonder as to the connection (or lack of connection) between Void and Metal.

There is no evidence to suggest that the Heian kata are linked to the 5 Elements of this kind of thought, but it makes for an interesting exercise to ascribe different feeling to the kata.

Which element fits which kata? Look at the qualities of Wood; which kata fits here? Heian Shodan seems to possess simple direct movement and a rising pattern that reflects growth. It is our foundation (our root, if you will).

Heian Nidan might reflect Fire. It certainly seems passionate in the whipping movements of shutouke and the coiled hip and spring of the kick. Similar to the way flames lick and coil about the tinder they burn.

Is Heian Sandan about the Earth? Does it show powerful movements and landslide effects. Is it ponderous and mountainous?

Heian Yondan has the power and grace of Water. One moment tranquil and the next a torrent.

Does the jump in Heian Godan reflect committing one's self to the Void that is the 5th Element, from the 5th kata? Why no jumps in earlier kata? It wouldn't be hard to slip some in, so perhaps there is more to it (although there are Shorin Ryu versions of these same kata that posses no jumps whatsoever).

 void

The true reason for the distinction into five kata can never be known. There are no books telling us what the founders of these kata originally intended. There is only cultural context and background knowledge for us to make educated guesses from.

Kata as Meditation

As the *jutsu* forms of karate became popularised as **do** forms, theoretically, the object of training changed. Funakoshi sensei's idea was that Karate would be treated as *moving meditation* for the betterment of character. Yet the majority of those taking part could only see the older fighting method, and so the art became a split personality.

The idea that you can lose yourself in the performance of kata is laudable, and something that all practitioners should try. Some will argue that this method prevents fighting applications from being made part of the subconscious, but we would argue that it internalises the movements to the ultimate degree, leading the martial arts practitioner back to the idea of "becoming the movement" instead of "doing the movement". Isn't this one of Bruce Lee's maxim's—"*Don't think, feel.*"?

Kata performed hard and fast become internalised as combative movements which flow together.

Kata performed slowly and with the *idea* of fostering greater **ki** become a form of what-the-Chinese call "*Chi-Gung*". That is a life-enhancing exercise for healthy body and internal energy.

In today's society, when we have so much to worry about, and so many things wrong with the world, there is very little that can totally absorb us. Distractions abound. Maybe, just maybe, you can lose yourself for a time in training. It helps if that training has a pre-arranged form, something that you can just repeat, mindful of movement and betterment, yet slipping from being totally conscious. The Japanese have a word for the flash of inspiration and enlightenment that can be visited upon us at these times—SATORI.

There's no better way to leave you than that.

About the author

John Burke began training in Karate in 1981. He has had breaks in his training which has led to investigations into Aikido, and Taekwondo, but eventually led him back to Karate.

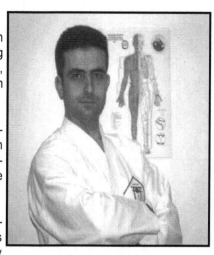

He has had a fortunate selection of teachers, always with what he needed at each point in his training, from the purely physical to the realistic, from the spiritual to the sporting.

John's first book, **Fortress Storming**, concentrated on the Bassai Dai kata and its applications, and was well received by martial artists. Also available are the beginners guide, **A Karate Primer**, and the book on the grading **Syllabus**.

Nowadays, John has featured in articles for *Martial Arts Illustrated* magazine and spend his time teaching Karate and Iaido, writing books and making tuition dvds.

His seminars are taught across Britain and internationally, and his students have clubs that form the Eikoku Karate-do Keikokai— an association dedicated to training incorporating the old ways.

A large amount of information is available from John's website, as are his other products, at
www.Bunkai.co.uk

Seminars with John Burke sensei are available internationally to cover

Traditional Karate, Kata Bunkai, Oyo, and Pressure Points.

For more information contact
01626 360 999
E-mail sensei@karateacademy.co.uk

Website www.karateacademy.co.uk

Regular training in the **Eikoku Karatedo Keikokai** under John Burke and his team of instructors can be undertaken across Devon

For an up to date list of venues and times in **Newton Abbot, Totnes, Paignton, and Torquay**, please see our website.

Video & DVD footage of tuition and seminars also available.

Also Available

Involving the same author.
Books:
Fortress Storming. Examining the Bassai kata, performance, and applications

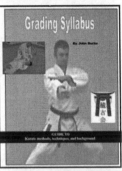

Grading Syllabus. The official syllabus for the Eikoku Karate-do Keikokai. Listing all the basics, Kumite, Kata, and Oyo that must be learned and providing guidance on Bunkai requirements for examinations.

A Karate Primer. Background, History, Philosophy, and sample applications for Karate practice.

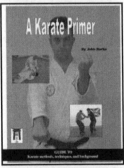

Fortress Storming—the Minor Version. Examining the performance and applications of the Bassai Sho kata.

DVDs
Syllabus dvds for the Eikoku Karate-do Keikokai for each grade:
White Belt
Orange Belt
Red Belt
Yellow Belt
Green Belt
Purple Belt
Purple & White Belt
Brown Belt
Brown—Brown & White Belt
Brown & Double White Belt

Kata Application series
Kihon
Heian Shodan

Heian Nidan
Heian Sandan
Heian Yondan
Heian Godan
Tekki Shodan
Bassai Dai
Jion

Seminar series
Nijushiho & Niseishi Kata Comparison
OCI 2003 double disc set.

Resources

Rather than a bibliography, I find that people provide more feedback and information. While good books are a great resource, good people can never be replaced. The number of books and articles that I have drawn reference from are innumerable, but the people who influence our development are easier to list:

Eikoku Karate-do Keikokai

This is the organisation of our karate, where application plays a major part in learning kata. The members are a terrific source of encouragement and inspiration, and without them this book would not exist.

The association is open to clubs to join, but potential instructors must be willing to be inspected and approved prior to membership being granted.

Information: www.karateacademy.co.uk
Association enquiries: info@karateacademy.co.uk
Training enquiries: sensei@karateacademy.co.uk
01626 360999

Open Circle Institute

The governing body and external verifiers association. Traditional martial arts with forward thinking. Renshi Anthony Blades is a great sensei in the true sense, and causes me to question everything that I discover.

www.opencircleinstitute.co.uk

Russell Stutely

The renown pressure point expert and founder of OCFM. Russell has a wealth of information and was responsible for the technology that put the pieces of the puzzle together in my head.

www.russellstutely.co.uk

Patrick McCarthy

Hanshi McCarthy is a valuable resource for the world of martial arts. His historical research and publications are groundbreaking. Without him much knowledge would not have come to light. Hanshi is the founder of the International Ryukyu Karate-jutsu Research Society.

www.koryu-uchinadi.com

KSL—The discussion forum of the International Ryukyu Karate-jutsu Research Society. The members of which have been a great help with assistance in translations and kanji information, let alone supporting individual learning.

EJMAS & Joe Swift

Another great source of information. www.ejmas.com

www.24fightingchickens.com

Rob Redmond's site provides much food for thought.

Classical Fighting Arts Magazine

Many of the articles have inspired parts of this book.www.dragon-tsunami.org/Cfa/Pages/cfahome.htm

www.russellstutely.com

Russell has been acknowledged as Europe's Leading Authority on the use of Acupressure Points in the Martial Arts. One of the leading sources of inspiration in street useable Kata Bunkai.

Over the last 8 years, Russell has been instrumental in dragging Traditional Martial Arts kicking and screaming into the 21st Century.

Never one to rest on his laurels he has continued to train and develop every aspect of Kata Bunkai, Self Defence and indeed the sporting applications of the Arts.

Russell is a regular Columnist for Britain's most prestigious Martial Arts magazines, Martial Arts Illustrated, Traditional Karate and Combat. He is in constant demand on the seminar circuit, teaching his proven methods of the correct use of Pressure Points in Kata Bunkai, The OCFM Syllabus and street applicable self defence.

Russell has been instrumental in the formulation of the OCFM Syllabus that has been ratified Worldwide. He is in constant demand on the Seminar Circuit and also for Private Classes and the ever more popular OCFM Courses.

"Russell is great to watch in action" Peter Consterdine ~ 7th Dan Karate

"Russell makes Pressure Points so easy to use. He has transformed my Martial Arts" ~ Bob Sykes 6th Dan Karate ~ Editor of Martial Arts Illustrated.

"Russell puts the reality back into Martial Arts" Rich Mooney 8th Degree Kung Fu

"Waveform strikes are amazingly powerful ~ I have never been hit so hard" Master Mark Adlington 4th Degree Tang Soo Do

"Real self defence, made real easy. Russell and the OCFM is where you should go if you want to learn what your Art really means" Malcolm Keith 3rd Dan Ju Jitsu

See the website for Special Offers

SEMINARS | COURSES | TRAINING CAMPS | DVD's | VIDEO's | PRIVATE CLASSES | GROUP CLASSES